DRINKING FROM a DRY WELL

DRINKING FROM a DRY WELL

Thomas H. Green, S.J.

AVE MARIA PRESS   Notre Dame, Indiana 46556

Imprimi potest
Rev. Amando S. Cruz, S.J.
Acting Provincial, Philippine Province
October 12, 1990

Nihil obstat
Msgr. Jose C. Abriol
Vicar General and Censor

Imprimatur
+ Jaime Cardinal L. Sin, D.D.
Archbishop of Manila
October 17, 1990

International Standard Book Number: 0-87793-451-7
0-87793-450-9 (pbk.)

Library of Congress Catalog Card Number: 90-85156

Cover design by Katherine Robinson Coleman.

Printed and bound in the United States of America.

Contents

Introduction

Drinking From a Dry Well is intended as a sequel to *When the Well Runs Dry*, written in 1979. In that earlier book I explored the transition from the meditative and affective prayer of beginners in the interior life to the dryness of mature prayer that St. John of the Cross calls the "dark night of the soul." This transition, John tells us, is the normal experience of all who persevere in a life of "mental" prayer. And yet, as he also affirms, very few do persevere in the dryness or darkness. Very few are willing to pay the price, to accept the cost of that purifying transformation that the Lord himself works in the dry darkness. Most pray-ers do not reject God, but they do settle for a level of comfortable mediocrity. They "work for God" (as I expressed it in *Darkness in the Marketplace*) rather than "doing God's work" — or, to put it more accurately, rather than allowing *him* to do his work in us. The purpose of *When the Well Runs Dry* was to help pray-ers (and myself) to understand and accept the challenge of living with dryness as the normal goal of a life of prayer.

Initially this dryness or darkness is truly disturbing. God, whom we have grown to love and desire, seems absent or at least silent. We fear that we may have offended him and perhaps even lost him. This was my own experience, and many of you have echoed it in the hundreds of letters I have received since the *Well* was published. You said that you felt that the book was speaking directly to you, and that you found great peace in the realization that what was happening in your life was a sign not of failure but of real growth. What a joy it was to learn that the Lord had so many good friends. The "very few" of whom John of the Cross speaks were many more than I had ever imagined — in all walks of life and in every part of the world.

As the years passed, however, I felt the need to return to the dry well, to ask what happens to the pray-er once he or she has come to be "at home" in the darkness. I am often asked whether the dark night (or dry well) is *always* a form of desolation. That is, is it necessarily disturbing? Does it always destroy our peace? At the beginning, yes, since we do not understand what is happening and we fear that we have lost the Lord. But if we persevere, and if we find good guidance from an understanding director or from spiritual masters such as John and Teresa, we can truly come to be at peace in the dark. We can learn to "float," as I expressed it in the *Well*. Our senses and our understanding find this dry darkness difficult and challenging. But there is an underlying confidence, born of obscure but firm faith, that "all things are well."

It is this new situation of "peace in the dark" that I wish to explore in the present book, written at my mother's apartment and with her unfailing support and encouragement, while on sabbatical from my ministry in the Philippines. Since my

own vocation — and that of the great majority of you readers
— is to be an active apostle in the church (a "contemplative in action"), we shall consider the experience of mature
dryness both in our prayer and in our active life. In Part
One I discuss what happens in formal prayer once the initial
struggle to accept the silence of God is over and the pray-er
learns to be at home in the dryness or darkness. In Part Two
I explore the implications of this new state for our active,
marketplace life. Hence the second part may also be seen as
a sequel to *Darkness in the Marketplace* (1981), which was
concerned with the link between the chapel and the marketplace, formal prayer and life "in the world," in the process of
transformation that John of the Cross called the dark night of
the soul.

John is the great master of mature prayer, and the first
part of the present book is based principally on his writings.
In the second part Ignatius Loyola, my father in the Lord and
one of the first founders of a fully apostolic community in
the church, is our guide. By a happy coincidence, 1991 is
the 400th anniversary of John's death and also the 500th of
Ignatius' birth. It is thus an important centennial for both the
Carmelites and the Jesuits. I consider it a privilege to be able
to dedicate this book to these two men who, "under God, have
been the fathers of my soul" (as St. Francis Xavier long ago
referred to Ignatius).

An important theme that emerged in the writing of the
book is that the spiritualities of John and of Ignatius, despite
their different charisms (contemplative and apostolic), are really remarkably similar in essence. The process of becoming
free from all disordered attachments in order to be *free for* God
in love and service is the heart of the matter for both of them.
And it is, as they make clear, the heart of Jesus' gospel teaching. May they bless this book and make it a good instrument,

9

an "instrument shaped to the hand of God" as Ignatius puts it, for transforming in love the women and men of our day.

August 6, 1990
The Feast of the Transfiguration

Shortly after I completed the above lines, and before I had a chance to send them off to the publisher, my own best friend, my mother, died peacefully in her sleep. The two of us had just returned from a beautiful five-day trip to the Adirondack Mountains. She was in great form, and we had many opportunities to reminisce and to share. One thing she said to me then (since reading had become more difficult for her, she used to listen to my cassettes to put her to sleep!) was that she wondered if she really knew how to pray. She went to Mass daily, and she did pray, but it seemed to her that her "way" was too easy, too direct. She was as comfortable with the Lord as with us, her family. Wasn't something wrong here?

I knew better. I knew her grief when my dad died in 1973. I knew, from her telling, of the struggles they had in the depression years when I was a small child. I knew of my dad's devotion to St. Jude, the patron of hopeless cases, from that Christmas Day in 1941 when his eldest brother, and my godfather, had committed suicide. No; her way was not too shallow, too easy. She had paid a high price — as all of us must — to come to the serenity of her eighty-fourth year. She had experienced what I am writing about in this book. As I write these lines, now alone in her suddenly empty apartment, my prayer to her is this: May she and my dad now help me, and all of you, to this same transforming peace.

August 26, 1990
The Day of My Mother's Transfiguration

PART ONE

In Prayer: The Vertical Dimension

---

1. Loving Attentiveness

Truth and Freedom

When Jesus came to the climactic moment of his life, the "hour" that had defined his words and his deeds from the beginning of his ministry (Jn 2:4), he spoke to Pilate of the reason for his very being: "You say that I am a king. For this I was born, and for this I have come into the world, to bear witness to the truth. Everyone who is of the truth hears my voice" (Jn 18:37). Pilate cannot, or will not, understand what this means; he dismisses Jesus' claim and ends the discussion with the infamous reply, "What is truth?"

Pilate's question, though, is not as shallow or as flippant as it might at first appear to be. What, indeed, *is* "truth" for the Jesus of St. John's gospel? The word recurs frequently in John, especially in the crucial confrontation between Jesus and the "Jews" (i.e., the scribes and Pharisees of the synoptic tradition) in chapters 5, 7, and 8. As John McKenzie tells us in

11

his classic *Dictionary of the Bible*, "truth" in the Old Testament is closely related to "faith." It is that which is solid, steadfast, unchanging — that in which one can believe. "The true is not merely an object of intellectual assent, but something that demands a personal commitment. In a sense one can be said to choose or accept the truth rather than assent to it." In the New Testament, the Hebrew sense of personal commitment is still present; now it is Jesus who witnesses to the truth, to whom the hearer is called to commit herself or himself.

To hear the truth, then, is to commit oneself to Jesus Christ. It involves not only the head but also, and even more, the heart and the will. Thus we can understand the deeper significance of Pilate's dismissive question. To listen to Jesus, and to enter into dialogue with him, would demand of Pilate (and the "world" he represents) an openness of heart, an acceptance, which would change his whole life.

But what of those who do choose to commit themselves to the truth that Jesus has come into the world to bear witness to? Is his truth clear to them? Since I write for such committed people, it is really their situation that concerns us here — and that led me to these background reflections. In John, chapter 13, there is a passage that suggests that this commitment to the truth of Jesus is not clear-cut, black and white for those who accept him. Rather, it seems to be obscure, groping, only gradually made clear: a commitment that involves tremendous trust in the person of Jesus. "Lord, to whom shall we go? You alone have the words of eternal life" (Jn 6:68).

Chapter 13 is John's account of the Last Supper. Characteristically, he does not describe the institution of the Eucharist as we would expect. Instead he narrates the story of Jesus washing the feet of his disciples, forcing us to look deeper and to discover the real meaning of the Eucharist. The Eucharist is, as the church's tradition has always recognized, the sacrament of Christian unity. We become one precisely by imitating the Lord in our humble service of one another:

"You call me Teacher and Lord; and you are right, for so I am. If I then, your Lord and Teacher, have washed your feet, you also ought to wash one another's feet. For I have given you an example, that you should also do as I have done to you" (Jn 13:13–15).

The incident that led Jesus to this profound teaching was his attempt to wash the feet of Peter. Peter objected. While it was customary in a desert land for the sandal-clad guests to have their feet washed at a party, this was the task of the servants and not of the master of the house. It is Jesus' reply to Peter's objection which I see as relevant to our whole life of loving commitment to the Lord and to his truth. He tells Peter: "What I am doing you do not know now, but afterward you will understand" (Jn 13:7). Peter must trust that the Lord knows what he is doing even if it does not make sense to Peter. Only later, much later perhaps, will he and the other disciples see the wisdom and the real meaning of Jesus' way of dealing with them.

When we think of it, this is the pattern of the whole gospel. Mary puzzles over the incidents recounted in Luke, chapters 1 and 2, storing them up in her heart until the paschal mystery brings their true meaning to light. Jesus' disciples frequently fail to understand his words and his works. Indeed, as we are told in Acts, chapter 1, on the day of the ascension, Jesus' final day on earth, their very last words to him are, "Lord, will you now restore the kingdom to Israel?" He has been teaching them and loving them for three years. It has been forty days since he rose triumphant over death, and yet they still do not understand the meaning of his life and teaching. They still expect a political messiah, a revolutionary leader in the Jewish tradition! Their only hope is Jesus' firm promise in the Last Supper discourse:

> "These things I have spoken to you, while I am still with you. But the Counselor, the Holy Spirit, whom the Father will send in my name, he will teach you all things, and bring to your remembrance all that I have said to you" (Jn 14:25–26).

Later, by the grace of the Holy Spirit, they will understand.

Prayer as Life

It has been twelve years since I wrote about maturing in prayer in *When the Well Runs Dry*. At that time I was struggling to understand the mysterious ways in which God had been working in my own life, and in the lives of some of the people I was privileged to direct. When I finished writing, I felt I had been able to "name," and to give some meaningful order to, many of the experiences of my preceding thirty years as a Jesuit pray-er and of my fifteen years of priestly ministry. But the whole history was still obscure and mysterious. I suppose I felt, not as if the darkness had been removed, but rather as if I could be at home with the darkness and at peace moving ahead in faith and trust. In the years that followed, I wrote about more tangible aspects of our life with the Lord: marketplace darkness, discernment as linking prayer to action, the dynamics of a good retreat in the Ignatian tradition, and the revolutionary vision of the lay vocation proclaimed by Vatican II. Still, in the depths of my heart, I knew that someday — if I lived long enough — I would have to return to the dry well. There was a wide gulf between chapters 4 and 5 (on learning to handle the dryness of the "dark night") and chapter 6 (on the goal of the long years lived in the dry well of prayer). This need to consider again the mystery of mature prayer was intensified by the extraordinary and quite unexpected reception of *When the Well Runs Dry*. The Lord had more dry-well friends all over the world than I had ever imagined.

So it is that we return now to the experience of darkness and dryness which I am convinced is the normal lot of those who are faithful to their life of prayer. Although we cannot fully understand this experience until we are able to see it whole from the other side of the grave, I think it should be possible now to understand better the mysterious process which leads from dryness to floating. We can pursue this deeper understanding in two steps: In the present chapter, allow me to summarize and rephrase what I now see to be the main insights of the *Well*; then, in the two chapters to follow, we will see what we can add in the light of later experience. That is, what happens when we come to be at home in the dryness or darkness . . . when we learn to live gracefully, day by day, by drinking from the dry well of prayer.

To begin, then, with a fundamental insight from the earlier book, let us recall that prayer is a form of life. As such, it must be dynamic and changing. Evolution has taught us that living things must be growing or dying. Change is the law of life. In the past ten years, the United States has entered a period of profound change, economically and socially. It is no longer the giant of the postwar years, straddling the world politically and dominating the economic order. The countries the U.S. interacts with — Japan, Germany and, most dramatically in recent years, Russia — are also changing. The great challenge for any American leader today is to adjust to these changes, and to lead the American people to respond creatively to the new challenges and new opportunities of a post-Cold War world.

Most people, however, resist change. It is easier, more comfortable, less challenging to sing the old songs, to play the game by the old rules. For example, we might see Gorbachev as a crypto-Stalin perpetuating the same Leninist-Stalinist dream of world domination, but now in a much more dangerous wolf-in-sheep's-clothing way. Or we may view what has happened in Russia as but a sign that the Cold War has been won: Communism has failed and capitalism has triumphed. In either case, we do not have to change our thinking, to grow.

Similarly in my world in the Philippines, ideologues of the right and the left alike are determined to fit President Cory Aquino and her government into their mental molds. To the far left she is just as "capitalist" and elitist as Marcos was. Corruption and repression are as bad as ever; only the cast of characters has changed while the script remains the same. And to the right she is worse than Marcos, soft on (and naively vulnerable to) communism and unrealistic in her hope of transforming the Philippine economic and political system into the only functioning democracy in Southeast Asia. The right and the left are diametrically opposed in their interpretation of the Philippines' "people power" revolution of 1986. The one thing they agree on is that the present situation can be absorbed into a pre-existing world view. Whatever change there may be is superficial. The old categories still hold.

The truth of the matter is that the world of the Philippines has changed with the advent of Cory Aquino, though not entirely, since, like all of us, she is influenced by her past. Cory is the widow of the murdered Ninoy Aquino. She trusted people because of their earlier participation in the fight to avenge Ninoy's death — and she has been betrayed by some of them. She herself has said that it has been difficult to realize that not everyone who fought the Marcos dictatorship really had the good of the Philippines at heart. Some had a private, self-aggrandizing agenda which became clear only after the 1986 revolution. For Cory herself, however, the changes in the Philippines have challenged her to continue growing even after her accession to the presidency.

My point is that new situations demand new ways of seeing and creative new responses. We have basic, enduring beliefs, but the real meaning of these beliefs, and their implications for our lives, unfold only gradually. Often this unfolding is painful, groping, obscure. Since prayer is a form of life, subject to life's law of growth, the pray-er cannot settle into a familiar pattern of comfortable mediocrity without regressing in his or her love of the Lord. What is beautifully appropriate in the first blush of young love is awkward or inauthentic in midlife or old age.

Three Stages of Growth in Prayer

A second key insight of the *Well* is that there are basically three stages in a healthy life of prayer. Using the analogy of human love, I described them as getting to know (the courtship period); from knowing to loving (the honeymoon); and from loving to truly loving (the long years of day-by-day married life after the honeymoon is over). We cannot love what we do not know. Thus the first stage, with the Lord as with a human lover, is getting to know the person we are drawn to love. There may well be infatuation at the beginning of a relationship. But infatuation is not love, precisely because we do not really know the object of our infatuation. We are in love with our own romantic fantasy rather than with the real person before us. The object of our "love" exists only in our own imagination. "Falling in love with love is falling for make-believe."

In reflecting on the three stages through which any loving relationship must pass, I have realized that they can also be described, and distinguished, in terms of what we seek in each. In the "getting to know" courtship stage described above, we seek *knowledge*: Who is this person I am drawn to love? What are his values? What would it mean to spend my life with her? This knowledge we seek is not only knowledge of the other person. I also seek to know myself. Who am I really? What am I seeking in life? What do I bring to this relationship? What would I have to change in myself in order to share my life happily and fruitfully with the person I am drawn to love?

As I see it, in this initial "getting to know" stage (which I discussed in *Opening to God*, especially in chapter 5), with God, as with a human friend, the real challenge is honest *self*-knowledge. Some have said that my analogy of human love is flawed because we cannot see and hear and touch God as we can a human lover. But tangibility does not necessarily ensure the success of human relationships. It seems to me, the number of really successful marriages, where the human partner is tangible enough, is probably about the same, proportionately, as the number of successful prayer lives. The problem in prayer is not the invisibility of God. Rather, in both prayer and human relationships, the cost of real self-knowledge is greater than most people are willing to pay. We cling to our illusions, and our ignorance, about our real selves.

For those who persevere in the courtship stage long enough to come to an initial honest knowledge of themselves and of the other person, the courtship eventually leads to the honeymoon. In terms of what we seek in the relationship, we could describe this as a transition from knowledge to *experience*. While we are always "getting to know" ourselves and each other as long as we live, knowledge is not the central value of this second stage. The relationship moves from the head (knowing) to the heart (experiencing, loving). We seek not insight but the joy of being with the one we love. The same transition takes place in our relationship to the Lord in prayer. Now we are not so inclined to reflect (for example, to meditate on the scriptures) as we were before. We are drawn simply to be present to him in love, to sit before him, to bask in his love.

This second stage is an easy one for the spiritual director, since prayer is spontaneous and joyful for the directee. There are only two things the director has to tell the directee at this time: first, that it is alright (in fact, good and proper) to let go of meditative prayer and simply to be present in love to the Lord. Praying, after all, is not thinking but loving. The whole purpose of the getting-to-know of meditative prayer is to lay a solid foundation for love. But the second point that has to be made is not as consoling or pleasant: The honeymoon will not last forever. While it seems as if we have really reached the ecstasy of perfect love, in truth we are just beginning. As in every marriage (and friendship), the honeymoon period will eventually come to an end, because what looks like true love on the honeymoon still contains a great deal of self-love. I love you, yes; but to a large extent this is because you fulfill *me* and all my desires. "All I ever longed for long ago was you."

What is wrong with this? As a beginning, it is right. There is real growth in discovering that I cannot fulfill myself, that I need to go out of myself in order to find my own happiness. But, good as this beginning may be, it is not yet true love. My "love" is still focused primarily on my own needs, my own fulfillment. This becomes clear when the honeymoon ends and we have to come to terms with the ordinary days (and years) of a relationship that does not always make me feel good and fulfilled. Then we begin to realize the true meaning of the "for better or worse" of the marriage vows. Strange as it may sound to a couple on their wedding day, we need the "worse" as much as the "better" in order to make love real. In the better we learn the joy of loving; in the worse we learn to love unselfishly. When things are difficult, when frictions and personality clashes arise, then we learn to love the other for his or her own sake. Not because I feel good about it (which at the moment I don't) but because the *other's* happiness and well-being are important to me.

Learning to Let Go

It would be nice if we could learn to love unselfishly without experiencing the "worse" of a relationship. But, in my experience, at least, this does not seem possible for us sin-scarred human beings. And because this seems to be equally true of our relationship with God, the third stage of a good prayer life is the "dry well" or, as St. John of the Cross says, the "dark night." It corresponds to the post-honeymoon stage of a good marriage (or of a growing and deepening friendship). In a maturing relationship, there are times of insight and of joyful experience, but there is also a new element: deadening routine and even friction as the darker sides of our personalities come into conflict. John of the Cross says that this is a critical moment in our relationship with the Lord. Many people who pray enter the dark night of prayer, but very few persevere through it, because they do not want to pay the price of growth. Normally they do not abandon prayer or God altogether. They remain "good" people. But they settle for a level of comfortable mediocrity: loving, but not too much; giving, but only within the comfortable limits they have set for themselves.

Mediocrity can happen in friendship or marriage because people are afraid that their partner will discover their dark side. This can happen in prayer too, because even though the Lord does not have a dark side, our own struggle with the deepening relationship becomes a problem. We need to risk total honesty with God. We need to let him reveal the truth about our darkness. Jesus proclaimed that the truth will set us free. His hearers, however, were unable to face the truth and win freedom. "Nevertheless, many even of the authorities believed in him, but for fear of the Pharisees they did not confess it, lest they should be put out of the synagogue: for they loved the praise of men more than the praise of God" (Jn 12:42–43). Lest we think of the Pharisees as evil men, professed enemies of God and of goodness, recall that Jesus says of them earlier (Jn 5:39–40): "You search the scriptures, because you think that in them you have eternal life; and it is they that bear witness to me; yet you refuse to come to me that you may have life." Why then do they refuse to accept the call of Jesus to grow toward true life? The Lord himself answers the question: "It is because you cannot bear to hear my word" (Jn 8:43). They seek the truth and they desire the freedom of eternal life, and yet they cannot risk standing naked before the Lord. Radical, naked honesty is too great a risk for them — and for most of us.

I suggested in the *Well* (chapter 3) that the Lord normally leads us gradually into the dry-well stage of our life of prayer and love. There is a transitory stage of on-and-off dryness. At times God is close, and prayer is easy and joyful. At other times, however, he seems far away. Our prayer is empty, sometimes blank and sometimes filled with distractions. The important feature of this transition from the honeymoon to the dry well is its unpredictability. We never know what to expect when we come to prayer, and the expectations we have are usually frustrated. On Easter Sunday or our birthday or some other significant anniversary, when we expect a festival with the Lord, he seems to be a million miles away. But on the most routine of days, or at a time when we are discouraged and anxious, we find at prayer that the heavens exult with joy.

I said the most important feature of the transitional stage is this very unpredictability. Why? Because the purpose of the

21

transition is to teach us to "let go and let God." We cannot control the rhythm of his comings and goings. Before, we were quite active in prayer, and its fruitfulness seemed to depend much on our fidelity and our efforts. God seemed willing to dance to our music. Now, however, he becomes a more elusive lover. It seems that God now feels that we can pass from the milk of children to the solid food of adults (Heb 5:13–14), from being fed what we desire whenever we cry for it to receiving from the Lord what *he* knows to be for our growth and our real good. As with children being weaned, the process is usually gentle and gradual. Otherwise we might rebel, give up in discouragement. As John of the Cross tells us, many pray-ers do give up. They refuse to take the radical risk involved in letting go of their own control of what happens, and in letting God take over. If they are of an activist temperament, they keep control by abandoning the dry prayer for good works. The very goodness of works such as social justice masks the fact that they are "working for God" (doing for God what *they* wish to do) rather than "doing God's work" (allowing God to work through them as *he* desires). For more passive, "contemplative" types, the way to keep control, to work for God, involves filling their prayer with devotions, novenas, lists of intentions. In this way they keep talking, and so they avoid the painful dryness and silence that confront the listener.

The Transformation Stage

The challenge of growth was the main concern I addressed in *When the Well Runs Dry.* I believe John of the Cross is right in saying that most people who pray encounter the third stage of dryness (at least its transitory introduction) but very few persevere in living it. While remaining good and sincere, they are afraid to pay the price of growth. In fact, I suspect that every pray-er — even as great-hearted a soul as the Little Flower — finds the leap of faith demanded to persevere in the dark night or dry well a fearsome challenge. They need encouragement and some insight into what the Lord is doing. Otherwise they will become discouraged and lose their way. Of course, the Lord himself can and does provide this insight, this encouragement. Normally, however, God chooses to work sacramentally, through human instruments.

The problem is that the intermittent dryness of the transitory stage gradually becomes our normal, "permanent" state. Once we learn to let go and let God control the rhythm of our prayer experience, then the dryness becomes more and more the normal pattern. The oases of insight and of joyful experience become rarer, few and far between. We begin to suspect, fearfully, that this dry well or dark night is not just a passing phase of our prayer. In fact, when pray-ers who have entered this third stage ask me anxiously how long it will last, I usually reply, "How long do you plan to live?" That is not very consoling for someone in the dark night, but it is the truth.

Fortunately, though, as I hope to show in the following chapters, we can come to be at home in the dryness or darkness. This, in fact, is the main lesson I have learned in the past twelve years. But it will continue to be dark. While we might spend two to three years in the getting-to-know stage, where knowledge of God and self is the primary focus and fruit of our prayer, and five to seven years in the honeymoon stage, where loving experience is the dominant characteristic, we can expect this third stage of dryness and darkness to last as long as we live — if, that is, we are courageous enough to respond to grace and persevere in the dryness.

The main purpose of chapters 4 and 5 of *When the Well Runs Dry* was to encourage those whom the Lord has thus called to mature in their life of prayer: to help them to realize that what is happening in them is normal and good, though painful; to explain the signs John of the Cross gives us, by which we can distinguish a genuine call to live in the darkness of the dry well from a dryness due to our own negligence or to illness; and to advise them on how to cooperate with the dryness. On the last point, John counsels us to have a good and understanding spiritual director, and to trust his or her judgment that the darkness is really God's will for us, even though it may seem to us that we have lost him because of our own sinfulness. This is crucial advice, since in the early stages of the dry well it will seem as if we have been abandoned by the Lord we so much desire. At this time up is down, dark is light, and absence is encounter. We can scarcely be good interpreters of our own paradoxical experience.

John also advises us to let go of our own activity in prayer and to be content with a simple "loving attentiveness" to what God is doing, to cease trying to meditate or even to stir up our own feelings of love for the Lord. These efforts of ours won't work now anyway. And we will only interfere with what God is doing in us, and add to our own frustration. In the *Well* I explained this mysterious advice of John by means of Jeremiah's beautiful metaphor of the potter and the clay (Jer 18:1–6). We could also use the image of undergoing surgery. When we are on the operating table, the doctor anesthetizes us. He renders us unconscious precisely in order to save our life. If the patient were conscious during an appendectomy, he would interfere with the operation, trying to help or to protect himself. By "knocking him out," the surgeon is able to get on with the business of saving his life.

The surgery analogy also brings out another important point. You do not judge the fruitfulness of the operation by the feelings the patient had while on the operating table. He was unconscious! Suppose you visited him in the recovery room and asked how the surgery went, and he replied, "Oh, the operation was a failure! I was unconscious the whole time. Since I cannot recall a thing that happened, I will have to undergo the surgery again." How would you answer him? I know what I would say: "Good heavens! Don't judge the operation by how you felt at the time. See whether or not you have an incision. Check whether the pain and nausea that preceded the operation are gone." That is, judge by the *fruits*.

The same is true of our dry prayer. Don't judge it by how you felt during the prayer itself, but by the good fruits in your life. Do you find yourself more humble? More desirous of the good of others and the glory of God? More aware of your own sinfulness and yet more confident that the Lord accepts you as you are? As Teresa of Avila says, these are the signs of true love and of authentic prayer. If we see growth in these areas, then our prayer was good and fruitful even though it seemed dry and distracted to us.

Let us return, then, to our distinction among the three stages of prayer in terms of what we seek. We said that in the first stage we seek knowledge of God and of ouselves and in the second, experience. We can now see that in this third stage we seek *transformation*. The real fruit of our prayer now is not insight or experience, good and gratifying as these may be. Rather, our dry-well prayer is the time we give the Lord to transform us. He is the surgeon and I am the patient. I have to have great confidence in his skill and concern, in order to entrust my life into his hands. But if I do trust him, then I will submit freely and as gracefully as possible to his work in me. And this work is a lifetime task. It will take that long for my heart to be stretched wide enough to contain the infinite God, as St. Augustine's beautiful metaphor describes it. John of the Cross says that for most people this work of transformation will be fully accomplished only in purgatory. But for the pray-er who perseveres, the dry well is itself purgatory. The Lord is accomplishing the work of our transformation by means of this dry darkness. Thus I sometimes say to frustrated denizens of the dry well, "You really have just two choices: You can pay now and enjoy later, or you can enjoy now and pay later! Sooner or later you have to be transformed in order to live eternal life." The only alternative is hell!

The beauty of submitting here and now to the Potter's molding, the Surgeon's operating, is that the transformation God works in me can benefit many others. If I wait for purgatory, I will not then be able to help other people. But if I allow the Lord to transform me now, I can be a more effective instrument of his love — what St. Ignatius Loyola calls an *"instrumentum conjunctum cum Deo,"* an instrument shaped to the contours of the hand of God.

We will return to this apostolic dimension of life in the dry well in the second part of this book. Perhaps we could conclude this first chapter, though, with a word about the "loving attentiveness" that John of the Cross recommends to the pray-er in this stage (*The Ascent of Mount Carmel*, Book II, chapter 12, paragraph 8). He says that he or she should simply "abide in . . . quietude with a loving attentiveness to God and pay no heed to the imagination and its work." This is easy enough to do during the honeymoon stage, when God's presence is strongly experienced and we want nothing more than to be lovingly attentive to him. But what do we do when God seems absent and prayer is painfully empty? We cannot be lovingly attentive to him then. Or can we?

I think we can, provided we speak of attentiveness not to the Lord himself (since he seems far away), but rather to what God is doing *in us*. That is, to the dryness and darkness which we believe to be God's hand upon us. I often say to pray-ers who ask me how to handle this painful dryness, "If the Lord makes it dark, you make it darker." That sounds strange. What I mean, though, is to trust the Potter, to lean in the direction in which the Spirit is blowing. Don't resist his drying wind by trying to recapture the thoughts and rekindle the feelings of earlier days. Trust God that he knows what he is doing, even if we don't. And relax in his hands. In the chapters that follow, I hope to show that this is the way to become at home in the dark — and to learn to drink from a dry well.

2. Two Dark Nights

Five Types of Darkness

In my course on apostolic spirituality, one of the reflection questions I propose to my students is this: Suppose someone came to you and said that her prayer is "dry." How could you determine what she means by "dryness," in order to give her the proper advice for dealing with it? Let us consider this question now, by way of summarizing what we have seen in the preceding chapter. At the same time, we can set the stage for a fuller discussion of the deeper dryness that St. John of the Cross calls the "dark night."

As I see it, we can distingish five possible types of dryness to which our imaginary directee might be referring. To a beginner in the life of prayer, "dry" might simply mean not yet knowing how to pray. In giving a parish Lenten retreat recently, I asked the parishioners to spend twenty to thirty minutes after my talk reflecting on and praying over the theme I had discussed. Then we came together again for a brief summary and a concluding hymn. I explained to them the first night that no one would ever be sanctified by listening to me, that they needed to encounter the Lord personally, and that my role was merely to facilitate this encounter. I knew that if I asked them to do the prayerful reflection later at home, most would never find the time for it. At the reception ending the retreat, I was particularly gratified when one of the men told me his experience. The first night he was very apprehensive about having to spend thirty minutes by himself. But as the days passed, that time became the most fruitful part of the retreat for him. He discovered that, with the help of the conference and of the scripture passages I suggested, he could indeed encounter the Lord in the silence of his own heart. In fact, he looked forward to continuing the practice after the retreat.

This, then, is the first possible kind of dryness: that of the beginner who simply does not know how to pray (in the traditional sense of "mental prayer"). A good guide who can initiate generous beginners into some of the time-tested techniques for getting to know the Lord and themselves will be helpful in overcoming this dryness.

Suppose, however, that our imaginary directee already has a prayer life. She has learned the techniques and has found what helps her personally to a loving encounter with the Lord. Now, though, the techniques no longer work. She finds herself dry and distracted, whereas before personal prayer was an important and fruitful part of her life. This *might* be an exerience of what we have called the "dry well." But first we must check another possibility: It may be that her dryness is due to some negligence that has crept into her life. She may have grown careless in her fidelity to a daily time of prayer.

Or she may not be coming to prayer properly prepared and disposed. Maybe her very success in praying has made her think she can "tune in" to God whenever she wishes, without any self-disposing preparation for the encounter. Or the negligence may be in terms of some disordered attachment in her active life: a festering resentment over some hurt, a preoccupation with her own success in some endeavor, or a friendship that is competing with the Lord for the center of her attention.

How would we determine whether her dryness is caused by her own negligence rather than by the Lord's purifying hand? All of us are "negligent," in the sense that none of us, despite our generous desires, responds perfectly to the Lord's love. That type of negligence, however, is not a cause of dryness; rather, it is the very raw material (the potter's clay) on which God works in transforming us. So I would ask our imaginary directee to examine her conscience, to see whether any *new* infidelity has appeared in her prayer or in her dealings with others. If she finds many failings, but knows that they are all involuntary or were present earlier when the Lord was close and prayer was fruitful — then we can assume that negligence or a disordered attachment is not the cause of her present dryness. But if she does find some area of slippage — if, in the words of the angel to the Church at Ephesus, she has "fallen away from the love [she] had at first" (Rv 2:4) — then she should follow the advice of the angel: "Remember then from what you have fallen, repent and do the works you did at first." Removing the attachment or recapturing her earlier generous fidelity to prayer should also cure the dryness.

Assuming that she is not a beginner in prayer, and assuming no voluntary infidelity has crept into her life, the dryness or darkness of which she complains can be diagnosed as one of three types of positive dryness. First, it may be the transitional dryness of which we spoke in the preceding chapter —

on-and-off, unpredictable, alternating with times of consolation. In this case she should follow the advice we gave there: Let go and let God. Let him be the boss. Learn, in Teresa of Avila's beautiful words, to seek the God of consolations and not the consolations of God (*Interior Castle*, Fourth Mansion). Begin to learn to seek not beautiful insights or consoling experiences but transformation.

If, however, the dryness or darkness has become her normal experience over a long period of time, with only occasional, even rare, oases of consolation, then we are dealing with the more permanent positive dryness we call the dry well or the dark night, the stage that John of the Cross tells us all faithful pray-ers enter but very few are willing to endure to the end. It may begin with some apparently extraneous life crisis such as the death of a loved one, or menopause, or one of the other experiences I discussed in *Darkness in the Marketplace*. But when the dryness or darkness persists even after we have worked our way through the normal grieving process, then we have to look deeper to discover its real cause and meaning.

In Chapter One I summarized basic insights from the *Well* that can help the pray-er to come to terms with this initially traumatic experience. As I noted there, we can learn to be at home in the dark. Dryness or darkness is not necessarily desolation (absence of peace), though it seems that way when we begin this third and longest stage of a good prayer life. The most important factor in our learning to be at home with the dry well, of course, is our fidelity in living the experience over several years. But it is also a great help to understand (insofar as we can) what the Lord is doing and how we can best cooperate. John of the Cross is our ideal guide here. One of the greatest spiritual directors in the church's history, his particular charism was to assist pray-ers in their journey through the dark night. Let us try, in this chapter and the next, to translate John's teaching into contemporary language.

Nights Active and Passive

John of the Cross' *The Spiritual Canticle* is a lyrical summary of the whole sweep of the interior life. In *The Living Flame* he attempts, without great success, to "eff the ineffable," to describe the goal of the process of transformation when the pray-er is perfectly united to God. It seems that there is very little that even he can say about the time when God is "all in all." "Eye has not seen, nor ear heard, nor has it entered into the mind of man to conceive what God has prepared for those who love him" (1 Cor 2:9). The *Flame* is noteworthy, though, for its beautiful and striking imagery (especially that of the painful process by which a log of wood is transformed into fire, in Stanza 1, #19–24); for John's mature discussion of why it is that so few pray-ers reach the state of divine union in this life (Stanza 2, #27); and particularly for his classic discussion of the harm that an insensitive and narrow-minded director can cause to a soul in the dark night (Stanza 3, #30–62). Whereas the other two "blind guides" he discusses, the devil and the soul itself, merit three (#63–65) and two (#66–67) paragraphs, respectively, John devotes many pages to the danger of entrusting oneself to a director whose only goal is to form carbon copies of himself. He says that

> . . . it is very important that a person, desiring to advance in recollection and perfection, take care into whose hands he entrusts himself, for the disciple will become like the master, and as is the father so will be the son . . . for besides being learned and discreet, a director should have experience . . . of what true and pure spirit is (#30).

33

I reread this section from time to time — and I tremble. The work of direction is indeed an awesome responsibility. Fortunately, however, we have in John of the Cross himself perhaps the best guide a director and a mature pray-er could desire. His two major works, I believe, are *The Ascent of Mount Carmel* and *The Dark Night of the Soul*. John conceived of these two as a single book (for example, in Book I, chapter 1, #2 of the *Ascent* he refers to what is now the *Dark Night* as "Book Four" of the *Ascent*). And he addresses his teaching, somewhat misleadingly, to "beginners," by which he really means those who have arrived "at the time God commences to introduce them into the state of contemplation" (*Ascent*, I, 1, #3; see also II, 6, #8; II, 7, #13; and II, 2, #1–2). He apparently felt there were already enough good books available to guide those still in the earlier meditative and affective stages (which he considered an essential foundation) of their life of prayer.

The "state of contemplation" of which John speaks corresponds to what I have called the dry well. It is the time when God begins to take over the work of prayer, when the pray-er does less and less and the Lord himself more and more. John calls the whole experience a "dark night." And he makes clear that the pray-er is not simply passive (like a rock sinking in the water) but rather receptive, responsive — like the partner in a dance or, in the imagery I used in chapter 6 of the *Well*, like a floater responding actively to the wind and the waves on the sea of the Lord. For this reason he distinguishes an "active" and a "passive" night in contemplative prayer. They are not really two distinct phases, but rather two aspects of the same experience: two sides, as it were, of the same hand. As Ruth Burrows and others have noted, the passive night refers to what God does to effect our transformation, while the active night refers to our role in cooperating with his transforming work in us.

Clearly the passive night is the more important. That is, God's work is much more valuable than ours. He makes it dry or dark. He burns out of us all the impurities that, in John's beautiful image, prevent the log of wood from being transformed into fire. But he does not force our freedom. He does not effect our transformation without our consent and cooperation. Thus in the *Ascent* John explains how we can assist this divine work. Although it is a lengthy book, we can summarize John's doctrine of cooperation in one sentence: As the Lord draws us into the darkness, we should let go of everything that is not God.

At the level of sense (Book I), we should let go of all the body's "appetites." John says:

> We are not discussing the mere lack of things; this lack will not denude the soul, if it craves for all these objects. We are dealing with the denudation of the soul's appetites and gratifications; this is what leaves it free and empty of all things, even though it possesses them. Since the things of the world cannot enter the soul, they are not in themselves an encumbrance or harm to it; rather, it is the will and appetite dwelling within it that causes the damage (I, 3, #4).

John of the Cross is generally considered to be the greatest poet Spain has produced. Like any true poet he was a man of keen sensitivity to the beauties of creation and a great lover of nature. Moreover, he states clearly (for example in Book II, chapter 12, #5 of the *Ascent*) that the use of our natural senses and faculties is essential for beginners in the interior life. His point in the above quotation, however, is that the time comes when these "ways of beginners" must be abandoned. And the right time to do so is when they no longer help us to encounter

God. In his own poem, on which he is commenting in *The Spiritual Canticle*, John has these beautiful lines (Stanza 6):

> Ah, who has the power to heal me?
> Now wholly surrender yourself!
> Do not send me any more messengers,
> They cannot tell me what I need to hear.

When the "messengers" (the beauties of nature, joy in the love of friends, our favorite hymns and scripture passages) no longer tell us what we need to hear — then, and only then, should we abandon them in our prayer.

But why should we do so? If all these creatures are good, as John clearly affirms, why are they not good *for us* at this stage in our prayer life? John's answer is twofold. In the first place, these are not God himself. Lovely as they are, they are but creatures, shadow images of their Creator. And now (like the matchmaker or the friend of the bridegroom) they have done their job. They have brought us to their Maker. Once God desires to encounter us directly and personally (which is what John means by contemplative prayer or the dark night), they must, like John the Baptist, fade out of the picture. The bride must come face to face with the Bridegroom, without any intermediaries.

This is, however, not the whole story. John says that in heaven we will be whole human beings, not angels. We will love God with every part of ourselves, sense as well as spirit. Like planets orbiting around the sun, all created reality will be part of our solar system centered on God. The problem here and now is that our loves are not ordered. When John speaks of "appetites and gratifications" in the passage cited above, he means what St. Ignatius Loyola calls "disordered attachments." It is not our love for friends that "causes the damage" of which John speaks. It is rather the fact that these loves are *disordered*. And John is convinced (correctly, in my experience) that there is *some* disorder in even the noblest of our loves (I, 11, #2). That is why the Lord has to tell us: "Absent thee from felicity a while." The planets in our solar system do not stay tranquilly in orbit around the Sun of God. They compete with the center, and in so doing they destroy the harmony of our universe.

Of course, we may not be able to recognize this disorder. We may think God is really our center and these other loves are no problem. That is why the passive night (what God does to strip us of these attachments) is the more crucial. He *knows* when and where there is disorder in our loves. If we are to grow, we have to trust his judgment — and cooperate with his work of "denudation." And that demands *radical* trust. It would not be so hard to accept the Lord's removing from our lives friendships that were obviously evil, attachments that were clearly disordered. But our faith is put to the test when his two-edged sword cuts into what we value most and love best. Then it is truly difficult, even heroic, to cooperate with him.

Nights of Sense and Spirit

St. John of the Cross was trained in the Thomistic tradition of his day, as Pope John Paul II pointed out in his doctoral dissertation on Book II of *The Ascent of Mount Carmel*. He divides the human soul into sense and spirit. As a good Thomist, by the "spirit" he means the faculties of memory, understanding, and will. Thus the dark night of contemplation must purify and transform not only our sensible faculties but also these interior faculties of our soul. Indeed, for John this latter is the crucial transformation. He says,

> This night, which we say is contemplation, causes two kinds of darkness or purgation in spiritual persons according to the two parts of the soul, the sensory and

37

the spiritual. Hence the one night of purgation will be sensory, by which the senses are purged and accommodated to the spirit; and the other...will be spiritual, by which the spirit is purged and denuded as well as accommodated and prepared for union with God through love (*Dark Night* I, 8, #1).

John adds that the night of sense is "common and happens to many," whereas the night of spirit "is the lot of very few." The reason, of course, is because few pray-ers are willing to persevere in the journey through the dark night of their senses. Most cling to their attachments to persons and places, to nature, to their own comfortable way of living and praying. The charismatic, for example, may find it very difficult to surrender the strong feelings, and the ambience that produces them, of his community prayer meetings, even when the Lord seems to be drawing him to silence and solitude. And the law-and-order person clings to the familiar structures which give her security, although God now wishes her to launch out into the unknown.

These examples are particularly apt, since the attachments that block the pray-er's growth now will not normally be to things that are evil or obviously sinful. We are speaking of souls who have made a basic commitment of their lives to the Lord. They have rejected deliberate grave sin and even, for the most part, deliberate venial sin. Yet, John says, they can still be prevented from growing — by their attachment to the good! We have all heard the saying: "The good is the enemy of the better." But how can it be that a desire to praise the Lord, or zeal for his law, could be an obstacle to his transforming work in us?

John uses a now-famous metaphor to explain his point here. He first says that "Sporadic venial sins and imperfections that do not result from habitual practice...will not hinder a man as much as his attachment to something . . . even though the imperfection may be very small." And then, to illustrate his point, he says: "It makes little difference whether a bird is tied by a thin thread or by a cord. For even if tied by thread, the bird will be prevented from taking off just as surely as if it were tied by cord. . . . Admittedly, the thread is easier to rend, but no matter how easily this may be done, the bird will not fly away without first doing so" (*Ascent* I, 11, #4). The cord is deliberate sin, and the thread is some disordered attachment. As I explain the metaphor to people, it does make a difference which one the bird (the pray-er) is tied by, if all he desires is to walk about on the ground of mediocrity. In that case the thread will not restrict his movement, whereas the cord will be too heavy for the bird to pull. But if the bird wishes to fly to God, then the thread of attachment is just as much an impediment as the cord of deliberate sin. Whether tethered by cord or by thread, the bird cannot fly.

But, you might ask, how can my devotion to a way of praying or to the laws and customs of the church be a "thread" in John's sense? Since these are good things, how can we speak of *disordered* attachments here? For John these are crucial questions: They lead the pray-er into the very depths of the dark night. My "attachment" in these cases (if indeed we can call it an attachment) is not to sensible gratifications but to the goods of the spirit: to my understanding of what is right and proper; to my memory of the blessings of the Lord in my history; to my will (my desire) to cling to God and his will. What could be wrong with this?

For John of the Cross they are indeed attachments, at least until our spirit has been purified and transformed. And it is because the word "my" looms large in all of them: *my* understanding, *my* memory, *my* will. There is still a subtle struggle here to bring the Lord to dance to my music, to make God conform to my ways of seeing things. Because it is so subtle, it is particularly dangerous for the soul seeking divine union. It calls for the deepest and most soul-wrenching surrender of all. This is why, for John, the goods of the spirit, and especially those that center on God, are a greater obstacle to growth for the mature pray-er than are the goods of sense. The self-love contained in our attachment to the latter is more obvious. With the former, the attachment to self is masked and disguised as a desire for the glory of God. Is it any wonder that very few successfully traverse the minefield of transformation in this life? Or that John spends the whole of books II and III of the *Ascent* on the night of the spirit?

Since this topic is obscure and mysterious, a personal example might help. I became a writer of spiritual books by accident. But even though I had not planned on such an apostolate, once it began it naturally acquired a momentum of its own. One book led to more books; books led to lectures and letters from people seeking direction. There was success in a ministry I had not anticipated succeeding at. And this led to certain dangers. I could easily get a "swelled head" because of the praises of those who were helped by the books. I could develop a messianic complex about my spiritual ministry, a sense of infallibility concerning my pronouncements on prayer, and a desire to mold my directees according to my own apparently correct ideas. I could, in short, become the kind of director against whom John rails in Book III of *The Living Flame of Love*!

These are dangers indeed, but I think they are fairly easily recognized as such. In John's classification, they are at the level of sense: They come from hearing praise, from seeing people grow in God. I do have to guard against them, but the temptation to disordered attachment is fairly obvious. There is, however, a more subtle danger of which I have to be aware. Although I try to pray my way through the writing of the books, there is always the temptation to say what *I* want to say — all for the glory of God, of course! — rather than to allow God to say through me whatever *he* wishes. It is all too easy to center on the project as *my* book, based on *my* understanding of how the Lord works and *my* memory of the experiences in which he has revealed his way, in order to fulfill *my* desire that people come to him. That is a danger against which I have to be ever vigilant. It is rooted in my very soul, something I have to wrestle with in my most private moments, and something not merely triggered by my encounters with others at the level of sense.

Rooting Sense in Spirit

In Chapter Three I hope to discuss in greater detail the mysterious process of transformation and our part in it, which is the dark night of the soul. But to conclude this contrast of John's two nights, let us consider an important passage in the *Dark Night* (II, 3, #1) where he explicitly links the two. The *Dark Night* is his discussion of the passive night, of what God does in purifying and transforming us. Book I deals with the night of sense; and here, at the beginning of Book II, John makes the transition from sense to spirit. He says that the purpose of the night of sense is that the senses "could be accommodated and united to the spirit." Naturally speaking, as St. Paul notes in Romans, we find two conflicting "laws" at work within us: Our instinctual nature struggles with the "inner man." At the level of sense we desire what gratifies our senses, and at the level of spirit we desire to please the Lord and do his will. "I do not understand my own actions. For I do not do what I want, but I do the very thing I hate....I can will what is right, but I cannot do it. For I do not do

41

the good I want, but the evil I do not want is what I do"
(Rom 7:15, 18–19).

What Paul is describing here is the universal human struggle between sense and spirit. John of the Cross tells us that
the purpose of the night of sense is to bring the senses into
harmony with the spirit "so that they could be accommodated
and united to the spirit." The fast of the senses that John describes — and which we have discussed earlier in this chapter
— has as its purpose to tame them, to conquer their tendency
to resist the spirit's desire to "do the good." It is a lengthy and
painful process. And, as every pray-er has probably discovered, the battle seems never completely won. Because of the
dryness and darkness of our prayer, we do gradually acquire a
greater mastery of our sensual nature. But there are still blind
spots and occasional lapses.

Does this mean that the night of sense has not yet accomplished its purpose in us? For John, surprisingly, the answer is
"No." What it indicates, instead, is that this night is only the
first part of an ongoing process. As John says in the passage
cited (II, 3, #1):

> One part is never adequately purged without the other.
> The real purgation of the senses begins with the spirit.
> Hence the night of the senses we explained should be
> called a certain reformation and bridling of the ap-
> petite rather than a purgation. The reason is that all
> the imperfections and disorders of the sensory part are
> rooted in the spirit and from it receive their strength.
> All good and evil habits reside in the spirit and, until
> these habits are purged, the senses cannot be com-
> pletely purged of their rebellions and vices.

We might explain John's point here by using the analogy
of weeding a garden. In the night of sense we cut the weeds
off at ground level. They no longer appear, so the garden

looks beautiful and well tended. But the trouble is that the roots are still there underground. Until they are uprooted, the weeds will surely reappear. Similarly, our sensible failings are just the surface manifestations of a deeper problem. We can chop away at them, but they will resurface unless and until the Lord digs out the roots in our "spirit," our interior faculties of memory, understanding, and will.

As we saw, John also calls the night of sense "a certain reformation and bridling of the appetite rather than a purgation." That is, in this first night the sensible appetites are brought into harmonious subordination to the will. They now work in tandem with our spiritual nature. But the problem is that the will (and understanding and memory) is itself not purified. There is, even in the best of us, a subtle self-love mingled with even our noblest loves and aspirations. And so, if we are generous enough to allow the Lord full freedom to transform us, his scalpel must cut deeper into the center of our soul.

The realization of what the Lord is doing in the darkness can bring peace to us. That is one of the principal purposes of this book. But I cannot deny that there is also pain. The very realization that the roots of our attachments, of our "sickness unto death," are far deeper than we had ever imagined—that realization itself can bring anguish and discouragement, even near despair. So before turning to a more detailed discussion of the transformation of our spiritual faculties, in the next chapter, let us draw encouragement from another famous metaphor used frequently by John of the Cross: the log being transformed into fire by the application of heat. He mentions it briefly twice in the *Ascent* (I, 11, #6 and II, 8, #2), and returns to it in the *Living Flame* (Stanza 1, #3–4 and 19 & 22). The most extensive development of the analogy, though, is in Book II, chapter 10 of the *Dark Night*.

While today we would have to update John's 16th-century interpretation of the physics of burning, his use of the metaphor is still wonderfully apt. He says that the "purgative and loving knowledge" of the dark night "has the same effect on a soul that fire has on a log of wood." The fire

> . . . when applied to wood, first dehumidifies it, dispelling all moisture and making it give off any water it contains; then it gradually turns the wood black, making it dark and ugly, and even causes it to emit a bad odor. . . . The fire brings to light and expels all those ugly and dark accidents which are contrary to fire.

This is one of my favorite images for God's transforming work in the dark night. When the fire of his Spirit touches and penetrates the log of wood which is the pray-er, the initial effect is painful and alarming. The damp wood gives off dense smoke. Then, as it dries, it turns black and ugly, and all its flaws are revealed as it cracks apart. Moreover, whatever maggots or worms are in the log come rushing out as they seek to escape the heat. If the log could think, it would say to itself: "This is a disaster! Far from becoming beautiful, I am much uglier than before. I have made a terrible mistake in submitting to the fire."

Of course, the log would be wrong. All the flaws and blemishes were there all along. The fire has merely brought into the open what was previously concealed: the moisture, the cracks, the maggots. The log's good self-image was an illusion. Now it is faced with the truth. And the truth will set it free! As John says, looking to the goal of the painful process of transformation:

> Finally, by heating and enkindling it from without, the fire transforms the wood into itself and makes it as beautiful as it is itself. Once transformed, the

wood no longer has any activity or passivity of its own. . . . For it possesses the properties and performs the actions of fire.

That is the freedom of the transformed children of God.

3. Seeing by Faith

The Challenge of Growth

In late 1985, President Marcos of the Philippines announced on American television that he was calling a "snap" election in early February of 1986. The venue of his announcement — the Sunday morning "This Week with David Brinkley" program — clearly indicated the audience he had in mind: the American government and U.S. public opinion. The Filipino people learned only indirectly of an event of critical importance to them. And they were to be given only three months, with a fragmented opposition and no organized political party ready to mount a campaign, to make their decision about prolonging Marcos' twenty-year rule. Despite this condescending treatment of the Filipinos (whom Marcos and his wife, over the years, had said were like children and had to be treated as such), and despite the massive fraud perpetrated

47

by the government to guarantee a victory for him, Marcos was defeated in the election. Then, when his rubber-stamp congress tried to rig the ballot count, the now-famous "People Power" revolution of late February sent Marcos into exile and brought his opponent, Cory Aquino, to power.

Mrs. Aquino is the daughter of a leading political family, and the widow of the man who, had he not been murdered by government operatives in 1983, was most likely to succeed Marcos. But she herself was not a politician. In fact, she had always avoided the limelight of public life. A reluctant candidate, she campaigned as a simple housewife whose one claim to fame was that she was the widow of Ninoy Aquino. She promised only honesty, integrity, and a hard struggle to clean up the corruption that had infected every area of Filipino public and private life. Ninoy had said years before that whoever succeeded Marcos faced an almost-impossible task. Recalling this, she told the people that cleaning up the mess would be a long, slow process. She invited them to join her in a crusade fraught with risk and demanding sacrifice, promising only that she would risk and sacrifice at least as much as they.

More than four years have passed since Cory became president of the Philippines. She has kept her promise. But, while most of the Filipinos still support her, it has become clear that many did not really want to pay the price of true freedom and justice. Many of the leaders of the opposition to Marcos wanted to change the players in the game, to get rid of Marcos and his corrupt family and hangers-on, but they did not want to change the rules of the game. This is where I see the "Cory phenomenon" as a parable for our discussion of the dark night of prayer.

We saw in Chapter One that prayer is life, and thus inevitably involves change. We must either grow or regress; we cannot stand still. We also saw that openness to growth means, inevitably, moving into the dry well or dark night of prayer. This is a daunting challenge. It involves submitting to a process of purification and transformation in which, as we saw in Chapter Two, we risk losing all the security blankets to which we naturally cling. John of the Cross is totally frank in laying out for us the risk, the cost of the crusade to which he calls us. Of course, John is not our real leader here. Jesus Christ has presented the challenge in the gospels and has spelled out the risks involved. But John is his inspired instrument in leading us to transformation in prayer.

Cory Aquino also sees herself as but an instrument of her Lord. She promised a just and free society — of, by, and for the Filipino people. Like her, John does not dwell exclusively on the cost involved. He promises us that "Finally, by heating and enkindling it from without, the fire transforms the wood into itself and makes it as beautiful as it is itself." This, of course, is the long-range goal, "finally" realized only at the end of our life. But there is a section in *The Ascent of Mount Carmel* in which John does speak of the positive aspect of our journey in darkness, not only at the end but also along the way. His discussion pertains to what I have called "learning to be at home in the dark." At the end of the journey, of course, all will be light. Only love will remain once we reach our goal in eternal life. As St. Paul says,

> Love never ends; as for prophecies, they will pass away; as for tongues, they will cease; as for knowledge, it will pass away. For our knowledge is imperfect and our prophecy is imperfect; but when the perfect comes, the imperfect will pass away" (1 Cor 13:8–10).

We could say that, for John, the dark night is the time when, even in this life, prophecy and tongues and "knowledge" pass away. As we have seen, that is what it means to live in the dark night or the dry well. And in the course of this chapter we will see that John warns us against trying to cling to any of these "childish ways," as Paul calls them in the very next verse: "When I was a child, I spoke like a child, thought like a child, reasoned like a child; when I became a man, I gave up childish ways" (1 Cor 13:11). What then is left to me? Is it "merely" darkness? Paul implies not, for he goes on to say, "For now we see in a mirror dimly, but then face to face. Now I know in part; then I shall understand fully, even as I have been fully understood. So faith, hope and love abide, these three; but the greatest of these is love" (1 Cor 13:12–13). Even after the sensible, perceptible "messengers" of God — knowledge and tongues and prophecy — pass away, we still see "in a mirror dimly" in this life. Faith is a way of seeing in the dark, and hope a way of possessing what is still beyond our reach. They are far from the perfect seeing and possessing which we long for, but they are also far better than the "childish ways" we have left behind us. This, as I see it, is the positive aspect of John of the Cross' teaching concerning the dark night. At least that is the beautiful message of encouragement that, in recent years, I have gleaned from books II and III of the *Ascent* (particularly chapters 1 to 9 of Book II), and which I would like to share with you in this chapter.

Accepting My Sinfulness

There are two sides to the experience of the dark night: It says something about myself *and* something about the Lord. The problem most generous pray-ers encounter is that they are overwhelmed by the realization of their own nothingness and sinfulness. They realize all too painfully that, as John says, the darkness of the dark night comes not because God (the flame) is dark, but because the soul (the log) is so ill-disposed to receive his light. (See, for example, the *Ascent*, II, 8, #6; the *Dark Night*, I, 8, #1; and *Spiritual Canticle*, Stanza 39, #12.) The dark night *is* contemplation or, as John often calls it, "mystical theology." It is dark not because the Lord is absent but because he is too present — too close, that is, to us sinners. Our eyes cannot stand his light. We are blinded by his brightness.

That realization alone should bring great consolation to the pray-er who fears she has lost the God she loves. Too often though, as we said above, she becomes fixated on her own "darkness" and nothingness. The devil enters in to convince her that she is hopeless, that her Lord could never find anything worth loving in her. How often pray-ers in this situation have said to me, with great seriousness, "Father, I am the greatest of all sinners." I know what they mean. And their humility is edifying. But I often have to puncture their somber balloon: "Why do you have to be outstanding? Why can't you be an ordinary sinner like the rest of us? After all, the Lord has known Genghis Khan and Stalin and Hitler. How can you claim to be a more outstanding sinner than they?" I do not mean to hurt their feelings. But their grim self-evaluation always reminds me of St. Teresa of Avila. She, too, was fond of referring to herself as the greatest of sinners. And, I suspect, that is why in a more reflective moment she offers this beautiful and famous advice to her readers: "Take God very seriously; but don't take yourself seriously at all."

We are very small beside the immensity of God. And considering his goodness to us, we can even see the point of Teresa's saying she was the "greatest" of sinners. In the light of his love for her, she could not imagine anyone else (even Genghis Khan) responding so poorly to God's personal love.

True enough. But the Lord has known our darkness all along, from the first moment he called us. *God* is not surprised or shocked by our sinfulness — *we* are! And the danger is that, with a kind of perverse pride, we can become fixated on this sinfulness, obsessed by it. If we are to grow in love, we have to accept the reality of our own sinful condition — even come to peace about it. Not because we like it, but because the Lord accepts and loves us as we are. He does wish to purify and transform us. But that is *his* work. We do not make ourselves worthy of his love by bewailing our sinfulness. Rather, he makes us worthy by loving us.

St. Paul tells us that "God shows his love for us in that while we were still sinners Christ died for us," and that "if while we were enemies we were reconciled to God by the death of his Son, much more, now that we are reconciled, shall we be saved by his life" (Rom 5:8,10). This insight is essential to John of the Cross' whole vision of the dark night. The work is God's, and contemplation (his purifying and blinding presence in us) is the means he uses to accomplish this blessed work. The "active" night is our response to him — not our initiative but our response to his initiative, as we saw in Chapter Two. A central component of this response is our humble acceptance of our sinfulness and nothingness. While desiring to grow, we must come to peaceful terms with the reality of who God is and who we are. This is the truth that will set us free.

Understanding Faith and Union

In addition to accepting our real situation before the Lord, in order to be "at home in the dark," we also need some understanding of what God is doing to bring about our transformation, and of how we can best cooperate in this work of love. We have already addressed these two points in a general way. The Lord is purifying us of our attachment to everything that is not himself. And what we must do is "let go and let God," like the trusting patient on the operating table. In the first nine chapters of Book II of the *Ascent*, however, John gives us a more detailed explanation of this process of transformation and of our part in it.

The central notions in his explanation are "faith" and "union," each of which he discusses in some detail after two brief introductory chapters contrasting the night of sense (already discussed in Book I) with the night of faith to be discussed here. "In the night of sense there is yet some light, because the intellect and reason remain and suffer no blindness. But this spiritual night of faith removes everything, both in the intellect and in the senses" (II, 1, #3). Thus the night of sense "resembles twilight," whereas faith "is comparable to midnight." The first night (of sense) is more external, as we have seen, whereas "The second, darker night of faith belongs to the rational, superior part; it is darker and more interior because it deprives this part of its rational light, or better, blinds it" (II, 2, #1 & 2).

After this summary review of his doctrine concerning the contrast between the two nights of sense and of spirit, John concludes chapter 2 with a list of the topics now to be considered: how "faith is night to the spirit," "the factors in opposition to this night," and "how a person prepares actively for entering it." If we can answer these questions, John believes, we will be able to cooperate better with the Lord's work of transformation.

First, then, what is faith? How is it "night" to the spirit? John begins chapter 3 with a theological definition: "Faith, the theologians say, is a certain and obscure habit of soul . . . obscure because it brings us to believe divinely revealed truths which transcend every natural light and infinitely exceed all human understanding." Like the sun swallowing up all the lesser lights of the night sky, "the light of faith in its abundance suppresses and overwhelms that of the intellect." Naturally, as John goes on to say (following St. Thomas and Aristotle), all our knowledge comes through the senses. But like a blind man being told about colors, who "since he never saw these colors would not have the means to make a judgment about them," so too faith "informs us of matters we have never seen or known . . . yet we come to know (them) through hearing, by believing what faith teaches us, blinding our natural light and bringing it into submission." So we believe because we hear (Rom 10:17) and accept the word of the One we hear, and not because we see with the eyes of our own understanding. "Faith, manifestly, is a dark night for man, but in this way it gives him light. The more darkness it brings upon him, the more light it sheds. For by blinding it illumines him."

This is John of the Cross' understanding of faith, which he proceeds to defend by citing several passages from scripture. As I see it now, the preceding paragraph provides the foundation for John's entire teaching concerning the active night of the spirit — that is, concerning what we must do to cooperate with the Lord's transforming work. He returns to the point in chapter 6:

> As we said, the soul is not united with God in this life through understanding, nor through enjoyment, nor through imagination, nor through any other sense; but only faith, hope and charity (according to the intellect, memory and will) can unite the soul with God in this life.

Our goal of union with God, a union that can be "total and permanent" only in heaven, is approached in this life only through an "obscure, . . . transient . . . likeness of love" between God and the soul (II, 5, #2 & 3). If God brings us into this dark night and unites us to himself, then we must cooperate by letting go of and renouncing every natural means, and by seeking him only by faith, hope, and love. What we need, in other words, is "a method of emptying and purifying the spiritual faculties of all that is not God" (II, 6, #6).

John reminds us again (#8) that he is addressing not beginners in prayer but "those especially who have begun to enter the state of contemplation," those whose prayer has become habitually dry and dark because the Lord is encountering them directly in the darkness of faith and no longer by means of sensible "messengers." *At this time* we should cooperate by "renouncing all that is not God." If he makes it dark, we should make it darker. We should try to dance to God's music even if we do not understand the words of the song or recognize the melody. This, for John, is the real meaning of self-denial.

Many "spiritual persons" misunderstand the true meaning of mortification.

> For they still feed and clothe their natural selves with spiritual feelings rather than divesting and denying themselves of these for God's sake. They think a denial of self in worldly matters is sufficient without an annihilation and purification of spiritual possessions (II, 7, #5).

They surrender money, comfort, material goods. This is not bad, provided such renunciation leads to greater spiritual freedom. But the crux of the matter is *spiritual* freedom. To be "pure as angels but proud as devils" is vice, not virtue. If my poverty makes me self-righteous, judgmental of others less poor, complacent before the all-holy God, then my poverty is a curse and not a blessing. My "spiritual possessions" (my own ideas of God and goodness, my consolations, even *my* desire for God) are what really block me from achieving true spiritual freedom. Only the self-denial that attacks these possessions can cooperate effectively with God's work of contemplative darkness. Only such a radical self-denial incarnates a living by pure faith.

John devotes the remainder of chapter 7, as well as chapters 8 and 9 of Book II, to proving this fundamental insight. Only self-denial understood in this radical, spiritual sense, he says, can make one a true disciple of Christ. And this is so because "no creature or knowledge comprehensible to the intellect can serve it as a proximate means for the divine union with God," as the title of chapter 8 expresses it. Hence "Faith [alone] is the proximate and proportionate means to the intellect for the attainment of the divine union of love" (II, 9, title). The terminology may be somewhat technical and theological, but this is because John realized how obscure and difficult it was to accept his teaching. And this not because of the terminology, but because his very subject matter is the dark experience of loving faith. He repeats himself, approaches the topic from every possible angle, in the hope that we his readers will eventually come to accept the truth of what he says. I know it has taken a long time for me (my head *and* my heart) to come to terms with it. But I am convinced that doing so is the critical breakthrough. Once we can accept and live by what John has to say in these few crucial chapters, we can learn to be at home in the dark. We can learn to ignore the thousand points of created light that seek to entice us, and to live solely by the dark light of true faith. Then we can cooperate effectively, and happily, with the Lord's transforming work in us.

Faith, Hope, and Charity

We have considered the first two questions posed by John of the Cross at the end of chapter 2 of Book II of the

Ascent: how faith is night to the spirit, and the factors in us that oppose this night. John's third topic, as we saw, is "how a person prepares actively for entering it." That is, concretely, how do we let go and let God? When God makes it dark, how do we make it darker? John answers this in the remainder of Book II (chapters 10 to 32) and in Book III. We saw that, for him, the "spirit" (as contrasted with the senses) corresponds to the interior faculties of the soul: intellect, memory, and will. Each of them must be darkened in the transforming process of the dry well. And this darkening or emptying is accomplished by the three theological virtues. "Faith causes a void of understanding in the intellect, hope begets an emptying of possessions in the memory, and charity produces the nakedness and emptiness of affection for all that is not God" (II, 6, #2). Each of these virtues or gifts of God, when received in its purity in the dark night, so fills the faculty in question with its brightness that it drives out all natural activity. In the same chapter John says: "If (the objects of faith) were manifest, there would be no faith. For though faith brings certitude to the intellect, it does not produce clarity, but only darkness." There is a dark and obscure certitude *that* God is and is lovingly present, without any clear, specific sense of *who* God really is or *what* he is doing.

Similarly, "Hope always pertains to the unpossessed object. If something were possessed there could no longer be hope for it. . . . As a result this virtue also occasions emptiness, since it is concerned with unpossessed things and not with the possessed object" (#3). And, "Charity, too, causes a void in the will regarding all things, since it obliges us to love God above everything. One has to withdraw his affection from all in order to center it wholly on God" (#4). Of course, we must always remember that this emptying is primarily and essentially God's work and not ours. It is not inhuman, though it might seem so to one who has not yet been captured by the love of Christ. To return to our analogy of human love, someone who has fallen in love thinks nothing of leaving family and friends to be with the beloved. The transforming love of God is certainly superhuman, supernatural, beyond our natural capacity. Here our analogy of human love fails us. Only God can leap across the infinite gulf between creature and Creator. Only God, to use the Augustinian image, can stretch our hearts (and minds and memories) so that they can contain his infinity. We can but cooperate freely with God's loving initiative.

This cooperation is, as we have noted before, what John means by the active night. In Book II he discusses how we can cooperate with the darkness of faith, by emptying our understanding (in prayer) of all that is not God. Chapter 10 is an enumeration of all the "apprehensions" of the intellect: natural and supernatural, exterior and interior, corporal and spiritual. Since the greatest danger to the pray-er in the dark night will be from "supernatural apprehensions" like visions, revelations, and voices (because these seem the most religious and godly), John spends most of his time (chapters 16 to 32) on them. The analysis is quite detailed, and very helpful to a spiritual director confronted with these phenomena in the lives of his directees. But John's teaching is really quite simple: Don't seek *any* of these! None of them is necessary to holiness, and preoccupation with them can easily lead the pray-er out of the darkness of contemplation. Are they genuine (i.e., from God)? They may be, in some cases. But don't pay attention to them anyway, and don't waste time determining which are genuine. If they are truly from the Lord, they produce their good effects during the very experience itself. Attending to them, analyzing their meaning, seeking to recapture or prolong the experiences is not helpful and can be harmful, because the devil can enter in thereby, fostering vanity and curiosity and filling our minds at the very time the Lord is seeking to empty them of all except his own transforming darkness.

In Book III of the *Ascent*, St. John gives a similarly detailed analysis of the various apprehensions of the memory (chapters 1 to 15) and the various feelings (joy, hope, sorrow, and fear) of the will. He never completes his discussion of the will, however; chapter 45 breaks off in mid-sentence. Why John never finished the *Ascent*, we do not know. But the loss is not great, since we can finish it for ourselves! The guiding principle for hope and love is the same as for faith: Do not cling to your memories or to your feelings. For example, do not be attached to places of prayer (chapter 38) or to private devotions (chapter 43). When the Lord places you in the "cloud of unknowing," as the author of the *Cloud* expressed it 200 years before John's day, fashion for yourself a "cloud of forgetting." Let go of the techniques for moving the feelings, those methods and practices that were useful when you began your life of prayer. What was help before is hindrance now, when the Lord is filling your faculties with the faith, hope, and love of contemplation.

Early in Book III, while speaking of the memory, John mentions three kinds of harm that can result from *not* emptying the memory, and three benefits to be obtained from doing so. Since they are typical of his whole argument, let us consider them briefly. First of all, if we cling to the memory in the dark night, there is harm "from the world," in that we are subject to many distractions and obstacles, such as vainglory (thinking ourselves "holy" because of our remembered experiences). There is also harm "from the devil," who can only work through our natural faculties, and thus is helpless and impotent as long as we keep our memories "in darkness and secure." Finally, there is what John calls "privative" harm: All these memories are an impediment to and deprive us of divine union, since "what the eye doesn't see, the heart doesn't want."

Conversely, the benefits of "forgetting" (parallel to the three kinds of harm just noted) are tranquillity and peace, as I realize that worry doesn't help anyway in the darkness of contemplation; freedom from the devil's temptations, since he can only work through the senses and so has no "handle" on the darkness; and, finally, a disposition to be moved freely by the Holy Spirit. The less I swim, the more I can float on the current of the Lord's ocean.

John of the Cross' Central Insight

Our purpose in this chapter has been to grasp the essential teaching of John of the Cross on the active night of the spirit. His writing is not speculative but essentially practical. John was a first-rate theologian and, according to the standards of his day, thoroughly knowledgeable in scripture and in the principles of scriptural exegesis. He uses this knowledge, however, not to construct a theological system but to provide direction in a very concrete situation: that of the pray-er who has begun to experience the dark night or dry well in prayer, and who does not understand what is happening or know how to respond to the challenge of the darkness. Different pray-ers, depending on their mental acumen and theological training, will understand more or less of John's explanations and "proofs." Some will understand very little. But, I feel sure, that would not bother John at all. He is a spiritual director above all else. What would matter to him is whether the pray-ers, who find themselves in the dark night he describes, can now go on to cooperate with the Lord's work in them more effectively and peacefully.

Ludwig Wittgenstein, one of my philosophical heroes and one of the twentieth century's most influential speculative and technical philosophers, has said in his *Philosophical Investigations* that good philosophy does not change reality. It leaves everything as it is. Its true fruit is not "knowledge of new facts," but rather a clearer picture of the situation which troubled us before we began to philosophize about it. This enables us to get on with the business of living well. The mark of good philosophy, Wittgenstein says, is that we can stop doing it when we wish and get on with life. John of the Cross would surely agree. If we get entangled in his terminology and his explanations, we defeat his very purpose in writing. We have simply cluttered our minds and hearts with more "messengers" who cannot tell us what we need to hear!

John would hope then that the readers/pray-ers he has in mind would be able to leave John and return to the Lord, now more at peace with their situation and better able to cooperate with his loving, purifying work in them. What would they now know? First, that the dark dryness of their prayer is not a sign of failure but of growth — that the darkness is evidence that the Lord is not absent but more present, and in a deeper way, than ever before. They should also realize that this is a critical, dangerous period in their life of prayer — that many (probably most) pray-ers lose their way at this point. They fail to grow, either because they misinterpret the dark dryness or because, understanding it, they do not wish to pay the price.

John hopes, of course, that his readers will be willing to pay the price. He says several times, in fact, that the role of a good director is to be firm but gentle with directees at this time. For example, in discussing the need to avoid seeking visions and supernatural messages, John says the director should never "show severity, displeasure or scorn in dealing with these souls" who are attracted to such phenomena. Rather, the director should...be kind and peaceful. He should give these souls encouragement and the opportunity of speaking about their experiences. [But then he] should guide them in the way of faith, by giving them good instruction on how to turn their eyes from all these things, and on their obligation to denude their appetite and spirit of these communications; [he] should explain how one act done in charity is more precious in God's sight than all the visions and communications possible... and how many who have not received these experiences are incomparably more advanced than others who have had many such (*Ascent* II, 22, #19).

A number of John's letters to his own directees survive; all of them reveal that, in the above lines, he has given us a portrait of himself as a director: lovingly concerned with the present situation of his directees, and yet firmly but gently drawing them, encouraging them to face the darkness and not be waylaid by anything less than the best.

If our reader/pray-er has been able to listen with the heart to John of the Cross, he or she now realizes that it is not ideas, memories, and desires in prayer that are the problem, but rather attachment to all of these. The Lord empties the soul of them precisely in order to free it of any attachment to created "messengers." So the pray-er's role (the active night) is to renounce, as far as possible, any attachment to insights, images, memorable experiences, ways and places of praying — in short, anything but the Lord himself. It is a question of sensitivity and good timing. As John says in speaking of the place of statues and images in our life of prayer:

Images will always help a person towards union with God, provided that he does not pay more attention to them than is necessary, and that he allows himself to soar — when God bestows the favor — from the painted image to the living God, in forgetfulness of all creatures and things pertaining to creatures" (*Ascent* III, 15, #2).

The same principle applies to every created reality; that is, our ideas, our memories, our desires by which our understanding, our memory, and our will cling to God.

What then is left? Only God himself, of course. But we encounter this God of ours in darkness. As John says, in speaking of the imagination's role at this time:

> The more spiritual a man is, the more he discontinues trying to make particular acts with his faculties, for he becomes engrossed in one general pure act. Once the faculties reach the end of their journey, they cease to work, just as a man ceases to walk when he reaches the end of his journey (*Ascent* II, 12, #6).

In what I have called the honeymoon stage, this resting in "one general pure act" can be quite fulfilling and peaceful, since there is a strong sense of God's mysterious, loving presence. Still, as John goes on to say:

> It is sad to see many disturb their soul when it desires to abide in this calm and repose of interior quietude.... Since these individuals do not understand the mystery of that new experience, they imagine themselves to be idle and doing nothing (#7–8).

That is the real danger in the early, consoling stages of contemplation: the sense that I should be *doing* something. But John tells us, "The advice proper to these individuals is that they must learn to abide in that quietude with a loving attentiveness to God and pay no heed to the imagination and its work."

At the beginning of the dark night, as John says, this "loving attentiveness" is both easy and difficult. Easy, because the pray-er is much drawn simply to be still before the Lord. But difficult, too, because of that nagging sense (fostered by the devil) that I should be *doing something*, that my "idleness" may be an insult to God. But once the pray-er is reassured that being lovingly attentive is all he or she must "do," then it becomes easy to rest in the presence of God. In the third stage, however, when the darkness becomes dry (or "arid," to use John's term) — that is, when God seems to be absent — how can we be "lovingly attentive" to him? This question long tormented me in my own prayer life. John gives the same advice ("be content simply with a loving and peaceful attentiveness to God") when speaking of the aridity of the dry well (*Dark Night* I, 10, #4). To me at that time such advice seemed like a cruel joke. How could I be lovingly attentive to Someone who seemed to be completely absent?

His other advice in chapter 10 made painful sense to me: Don't try to force meditative prayer; persevere patiently; trust in God. But what about that "loving and peaceful attentiveness"? How do you attend, lovingly or otherwise, to a spiritual black hole? Over the years I think I have found an answer. It seems to me now that what the pray-er must do is to attend lovingly *to the darkness itself*, convinced in faith that this darkness is the very presence of God. It is difficult to put into words, but it somehow involves gazing steadily into the darkness, not allowing our attention to be distracted by the thousand points of created light that seek to divert us from the darkness, hoping (sometimes against hope) that the very darkness will someday reveal itself as radiant light.

If this is hard to explain, it is even more difficult to live. But there are some signposts along the way (which we will consider in Part II) that tell us it is the right response, the meaning of John's "loving and peaceful attentiveness," for the pray-er seeking to drink from a dry well. If the darkness is really blinding light, could we not get water — the only true water — from a dry well? Jesus said to the Samaritan woman:

> "If you knew the gift of God, and who it is that is saying to you, 'Give me a drink,' you would have asked him and he would have given you living water." The woman said to him, "Sir, you have nothing to draw with, and the well is deep; where do you get that living water?"... Jesus said to her, "Everyone who drinks of this water will thirst again, but whoever drinks of the water that I shall give him will never thirst; the water that I shall give him will become in him a spring of water welling up to eternal life." The woman said to him, "Sir, give me this water, that I may not thirst, nor come here to draw" (Jn 4:10–15).

Darkness that is really light; dryness that is living water — our natural way of seeing and experiencing fails us here. We are left only with faith and hope and love. But gradually, mysteriously and incredibly, we come to discover even in this life that this darkness is the only true light, that only the apparently dry well can really slake our thirst.

PART TWO

In Loving Service: The Horizontal Dimension

---

4. Loving and Liking

The Second Arm of the Cross

In the literature of spirituality we often find references to "the interior life," implying a contrast between an inner life with God and an outer life lived in the world with our fellow human beings. In recent times, spiritual writers make a similar distinction between the horizontal and the vertical dimensions of our life in Christ. The horizontal, our interaction with the created world, must complement the vertical, our relationship with God. Like the cross of Jesus, there must be both horizontal and vertical beams. The implication in current writing is that earlier generations placed too much stress on the vertical, the "me and Jesus" dimension, to the neglect of the pray-er's involvement in the world.

There is a basis for this criticism. As I had occasion to note in *Come Down, Zacchaeus*, the third century's spirituality did involve a strong element of flight from the world. And, a thousand years later, Thomas à Kempis could lament, "Whenever I go among men, I return less a man." There is apparently a tension between the vertical and the horizontal, the inner and the outer, built into every Christian life. In his priestly prayer to the Father, even Jesus says,

> "I am not praying for the world but for those whom you have given me, for they are yours. . . . I have given them your word; and the world has hated them because they are not of the world even as I am not of the world" (Jn 17:9,15).

One could easily conclude from this (as many Christians have done) that there is an irreconcilable opposition between "the world" and the true disciples of Jesus, that one can live a truly godly life only by withdrawing from this hostile, sinful world.

The problem with this conclusion, of course, is that Jesus goes on to say in the very next verses:

> "I do not pray that you should take them out of the world, but that you should keep them from the evil one. . . . As you sent me into the world, so I have sent them into the world. And for their sake I consecrate myself, that they also may be consecrated in truth" (Jn 17:18–19).

Thus there is a built-in tension for every true disciple of Jesus Christ: They are "in but not of" the world. They are sent into the world, and yet they do not belong to the world. As we had occasion to explain in discussing the lay vocation in *Come Down, Zacchaeus*, true disciples cannot simply choose the vertical arm of the cross and reject the horizontal — not if they are to be authentic followers of Jesus. Their desire must be that of St. Augustine, so beautifully articulated in his *Confessions*: "I wish to do this truth before you alone by praising you, and before a multitude of witnesses by writing of you."

What, though, of St. John of the Cross? Does the horizontal arm play an important role in his spirituality too? We have taken him as our guide in maturing in prayer (the vertical arm of the cross) in Part One of this book. But what about our relationship to the world? Does not John's message (renunciation, detachment) seem to be almost totally negative here? I think not, if we have understood him correctly. In the first place, John has stressed that all creation is inherently good. What keeps us from God is not created reality (including human love), but rather our disordered attachments to creatures. The *"nada"* (nothing) of John, even in its deeper reaches which we discussed in Chapter 3, is not a rejection of creatures as bad or even worthless. It is, rather, an affirmation that all of them, good as they are, are not God. Since we tend to allow them to compete with God for the center of our lives, we need to get disentangled from our attachments and to allow the Lord alone to truly be our center.

Moreover, John does make clear that good works, service of the God of love, are important in his spirituality. He says, for example, "Thus through his good customs and virtues (the Christian) should fix his eyes only upon the service and honor of God" (*Ascent* III, 27 #4; see also III, 30, #5; III, 45, #4; and *Dark Night*, I, 2, #8). And in Book III of the *Dark Night* (19, #3), John discusses the third step of the "ladder of perfection" described by earlier spiritual writers:

> The third step of this loving ladder prompts the soul to the performance of works and gives it fervor that it might not fail. . . . On this step the soul thinks the great works it does for the Beloved are small; its

many works, few; the long time spent in His service, short. . . . Because of his intense love of God, a person at this stage feels deep sorrow and pain about the little he does for God, and if it were licit he would destroy himself a thousand times for God and be greatly consoled.

Finally, the "Sayings of Light and Love," which are preserved in John's own hand, begin with this magnificent prayer:

O my God and my delight, for your love I have also desired to give my soul to composing these sayings of light and love concerning you. Since, although I can express them in words, I do not have the works and virtues they imply (which is what pleases you more, O my Lord, than the words and wisdom they contain), may others, perhaps moved by them, go forward in your service and love — in which I am lacking.

"Works and virtues" are more important, more pleasing to the Lord than the "words and wisdom" of his sayings!

So the service of God in the world is obviously important to John of the Cross. Nonetheless, it is true that his references to it, clear and striking though they be, are not very numerous. This is not too surprising, however, if we recall John's particular charism as a writer. His vocation was to guide men and women to total union with God through prayer in the dark night. It was for this work that he was canonized and made a doctor of the church. Each of us accepts and tries to live the *whole* gospel. But Paul is not Peter, and neither of them is John. Each has a special work in the church. And each needs the others to "build up the whole Body of Christ." Similarly, I would like to suggest in the chapters to follow that John's great vision of the vertical dimension of our Christ-life needs to be complemented by an equally penetrating vision of the horizontal, apostolic dimension.

There are many great founders of apostolic orders and congregations. I happen to be a Jesuit, a member of the Society founded by St. Ignatius Loyola. That is the apostolic tradition I know best. But there are other reasons for choosing Ignatius as our guide in this second part of the book. The lives of John and Ignatius overlapped in a fascinating and somewhat mysterious way. Not only were many of Teresa of Avila's directors Jesuits; John himself was educated by the Jesuits at Medina del Campo in the years immediately following the death of Ignatius (also a Spaniard) in Rome. Ignatius died in 1556, when John was a young boy of 14. From 1559 to 1563, when he joined the Carmelites, John studied the humanities (our collegiate course) at the Jesuit college in his home town. The year of John's death, 1591, was the 100th since Ignatius' birth. Thus it is that we celebrate in 1991, by a happy coincidence, both the 500th anniversary of Ignatius' birth and the 400th of John's death. 1990 is also the 450th anniversary of the foundation of the Jesuits, who were thus barely twenty years old at the time when John of the Cross (then Juan de Yepes y Alvarez) came to study with them.

The conjunction of all these anniversaries is, in itself, merely an interesting historical coincidence. But I see a deeper significance in it — in my own life, first of all, but also in the history of the church's evolving spirituality. John and Ignatius had very different charisms, different roles in the church's life and mission. Yet, if we look deeper, they not only complement each other but share an almost identical vision of the essence of holiness. On the surface the differences are obvious. But if we look to the goal — the kind of person to be formed (one, Ignatius says, "crucified to the world, and to whom the world is crucified") — the spiritualities of John and Ignatius are remarkably similar.

John, as we have said, does not speak much of the apostolic dimension. That was not his particular charism, even though he does say that service of God is essential to true holiness. In Ignatius' lifetime, Jerome Nadal, whom Ignatius considered the authentic interpreter of his vision, described Ignatius' ideal as the "contemplative in action." Ignatius, however, has much more to say about "action" than about the contemplative dimension. His personal charism was to form apostles whose prayer and action were integrated to a hitherto unknown degree. Compared to John, he does not say much about the contemplative dimension — and specifically about maturing in prayer, which is John's great concern — as is perhaps most evident from the following: Over the centuries one common complaint about the *Spiritual Exercises* is that they are too mechanical, too "methodical." Even today, it seems to many, that "Jesuit prayer" never gets off the ground, that the bird cannot fly because it is tied by the threads of "preludes" and "points," of techniques of meditation and imaginative contemplation. What could be further from the simple loving attentiveness that John considers essential to real growth in love and holiness? It seems we have the Martha-Mary conflict all over again: on one side, bustling busyness in prayer and in action; on the other, blissful disengagement from all things in order to sit gazing at the Lord!

Persons and Projects

We have already made clear that "blissful disengagement" is not John's ideal, but rather a distortion of the detachment that he preaches. In the chapters to follow, I wish to show that "bustling busyness" is equally a distortion of the Ignatian ideal. Ignatius was clearly an organized, methodical person (unlike Teresa of Avila, whose magnificent side trips in her writing are legendary), but so was John. The writings of both of them attest clearly to this. Yet Ignatius, no less than John, saw the organization and the method as merely a means to true freedom of spirit. He begins his *Spiritual Exercises* with this guideline for the retreatant and the director:

> By the term "Spiritual Exercises" is meant every method of examination of conscience, of meditation, of contemplation, of vocal and mental prayer, and of other spiritual exercises that will be mentioned later. For just as taking a walk, journeying on foot and running are bodily exercises, so we call Spiritual Exercises every way of preparing and disposing the soul to rid itself of all inordinate attachments, and, after their removal, of seeking and finding the will of God in the disposition of our life for the salvation of our soul (Paragraph #1; see also #21).

The Spiritual Exercises, at least as Ignatius himself understands them, are not a fixed, strictly sequenced set of exercises. They are, rather, a sort of smorgasbord from which retreatants can select whatever helps them to the end in view: finding the will of God for them.

The end-means distinction is crucial to Ignatius' thinking. In his introduction to the first week of the Exercises (paragraph #23, entitled the "First Principle and Foundation,") he says: "Man is created to praise, reverence and serve God our Lord, and in this way to save his soul." That is his end. Furthermore, "The other things on the face of the earth are created for man to help him in attaining the end for which he is created." *Everything* else is means.

> Hence, man is to make use of them insofar as they help him in the attainment of his end, and he must rid himself of them insofar as they prove a hindrance to

73

him. . . . Our one desire and choice should be what is more conducive to the end for which we are created.

What could be closer in spirit to John of the Cross' "nada" doctrine? The essential visions of John and Ignatius are identical — total and unfettered centering on God and his will is the whole purpose of the spiritual life.

In *A Vacation With the Lord*, I had occasion to stress Ignatius' flexible vision of the Spiritual Exercises as but a means to an end. We have seen above that John and Ignatius have a very similar understanding of the reordering necessary to subordinate means to end. One significant difference, however, is the specific audience they address. John, in general, presupposed they were pray-ers who had already passed through the earlier stages of getting to know and learning to love the Lord. Ignatius, on the other hand, spoke primarily to generous persons beginning the journey of prayer and service. That is why he gives such detailed guidelines for each period of prayer during the Spiritual Exercises.

To be more precise, we should note that Ignatius gives these detailed directions only for the earlier days of the retreat, for what he calls the "first week," and for the first part of the "second week." By the time he comes to the fourth and final week, the text of the Exercises is only two or three pages long — briefer than the space devoted to a single meditation at the beginning. Ignatius obviously felt that, by the time retreatants came to the fourth week of the 30-day retreat, they would have discovered their own way of proceeding. Like a good John the Baptist, Ignatius can then fade into the background and leave the retreatant to encounter the Lord directly. Moreover, even in the Introductory Guidelines, Ignatius stresses flexibility and adaptation to the personal needs and situation of the retreatant: The director should be brief in presenting the matter for prayer, since "it is not much knowledge that fills and satisfies the

soul, but the intimate understanding and relish of the truth"
that comes from the retreatant's own encounter with the Lord
in the gospel (#2). Similarly, the four weeks of the Exercises
will vary in length, depending on the maturity, generosity, and
personal needs of the retreatant (#4). And the director has to
be very sensitive to what is happening between the retreatant
and the Lord, adapting his instructions and suggestions to the
person's concrete experience (#6 to #16).

Thus we can say in general that Ignatius' approach, like
John's, is person-centered. The Exercises are not intended as
a rigidly preconceived project, a procrustean bed into which
every retreatant must fit. There are indeed certain general
principles that apply to every prayer life and every pray-er,
because God is God and we are all sinful human beings. But
the unique situation of every individual retreatant is just as
important as these universal constants.

There is another, complementary sense in which Ignatius'
approach is strongly person-centered. Ignatius was one of the
most apostolic men who ever lived. But work, even work for
God, was not the be-all and end-all of his life and spirituality.
He was not a compulsive doer. What matters in the end is not
deeds but love — not how much I accomplish for God, but
the fact that it is done *for* him, out of love for him who has
loved me unto death. That is what makes Ignatius' apostolic
vision essentially contemplative. And this is precisely John
of the Cross' sense of "contemplation" as a direct encounter
with God in Christ Jesus.

This personalistic dimension of Ignatian spirituality can be
seen clearly in the four great thematic meditations that provide
frame and flow to the second week of the Exercises. The first
week has brought the retreatant face to face with his own
situation as sinful creature — totally dependent on God and
yet totally inadequate in living that dependency relationship.

The second week, which is the heart of the Spiritual Exercises, involves a shift of focus from self to God — specifically to God revealing himself and calling me in Jesus Christ. For Ignatius, the crucial point in every prayer period is the grace I seek, "*id quod volo.*" Throughout the second week, in all our contemplations of the gospel life of Jesus, this grace is the same:

> Third prelude. This is to ask for what I desire. Here it will be to ask for an intimate knowledge of our Lord, who has become man for me, that I may love Him more and follow Him more closely (#104).

To know God more intimately, in order that I may love him more ardently, and thus follow him more faithfully. Work (the "follow him more closely" of the text) is important for Ignatius, but only if it springs from deep knowledge and love of Jesus, and only because it incarnates my following of *him*.

It is in this context that the four great thematic meditations of the second week must be understood. At its beginning, the kingdom meditation presents us with the person of Christ the King (contrasted with an ideal human leader or king), and challenges us to respond to the call of such a loving, heroic, unselfish Leader — a call to follow him in the crusade for true justice and peace in the world. The goal (justice and peace) is important; but Ignatius finds the power of the call in the compelling personality of the Leader who calls us to follow him, not in an abstract ideal. Because we trust him and are inspired by his love, we have the courage to enlist in his crusade.

Similarly, toward the midpoint of the second week, Ignatius presents us with two further thematic meditations: the "two standards" or military banners, and the three kinds of persons. The former calls the disciple to discerning sensitivity, that he or she may remain under the banner of Christ (which has emblazoned on it "poverty, insults or contempt, humility," #146), and not be seduced by, or even drift inadvertently under, the banner of Satan ("riches, honors, pride"). Again, the call is not to embrace poverty, contempt or humility as abstract ideals. We are to see *Christ* calling us to these, and to respond by choosing his banner, precisely because he whom we love calls us to what, humanly, we recoil from. "Simon Peter answered him, 'Lord, to whom shall we go? You have the words of eternal life; and we have believed, and have come to know, that you are the Holy One of God'" (Jn 6:68–69).

The point of the meditation on the three kinds of persons is that there are levels of generosity in responding to the Lord's call and challenge. The first person wants to follow her Lord, but postpones making a decision because of attachments to persons and possessions. The second also wants to follow him, and realizes that she must act now or perhaps never; but she compromises. She wants to be free of her attachments, but she "wishes to do so in a way that she retains what she has acquired, so that God is to come to what she desires" (#154). She gives the Lord something, but it is what she chooses and not what he desires. She fears what love might cost in self-surrender. The third person places her whole life and all her possessions at the disposal of the Lord; she has been completely captured by the love of Christ.

I Write on My Knees

St. Ignatius must have been a magnetic, compelling personality. I recall my early years as a Jesuit, when he seemed dry and prosaic. Despite the magnificent ideals of the Spiritual Exercises and of the Jesuits' Constitutions that Ignatius gave to his Society, he was not a charismatic writer. Francis Xavier seemed a much more romantic figure, one I could relate to emotionally. During the years when Xavier was traversing the Orient — from India to Malacca to the Spice Islands to Japan and, finally, to a lonely but glamorous death on an island at the gate of China — Ignatius was home in Rome chained to a desk as the first Superior General of the Jesuits. Yet, from those earliest years of my Jesuit life, one fact intrigued and puzzled me: Xavier's magnificent love for Ignatius. In one of his frequent letters to Ignatius in Rome, he described himself as "kneeling on the ground as I write, as though I had you here present before me, *Padre mio de mi anima observantissimo*" (quoted in James Brodrick, S.J., *St. Francis Xavier*, p. 343). What was there about Ignatius that led Xavier to pen those moving words? I longed to find out for myself.

Eight years earlier, in 1541, when Xavier and his companions were preparing to sail from Portugal for the Orient, he had pleaded with Ignatius:

> For the love and service of God our Lord, we beg you to write and tell us at great length how we ought to deal with the infidels. . . . We pray and beseech you again and again, by the friendship which unites us so intimately in Christ Jesus, to give us your ideas and counsels as to the way we should proceed (Brodrick, p. 94).

Xavier loved Ignatius as "the father of my soul" (*Padre mio de mi anima*), and his love was reciprocated. In a letter written in January of 1552 (about ten months before his death) he recalls the way Ignatius had concluded an earlier letter to him: "Entirely yours, without power or possibility of ever forgetting you, Ignatio." Xavier says of these words: "I read them with tears, and with tears now write them, remembering the past and the great love which you always bore towards me" (Brodrick, p. 459). As the years passed I did come to discover why Xavier felt such great love for Ignatius. It became clear that, while the romantic deeds and heroic journeys were Xavier's, the *spirit* that animated them was that of Ignatius. He was the instrument used by the Lord to free Xavier for total love and service of Jesus Christ, his king. The banner of Christ guided Xavier to Japan and ultimately to the threshold of China. He desired to be Ignatius' third kind of person, a person prepared and disposed by the Spiritual Exercises (#1) "to rid itself of all inordinate attachments and, after their removal, to seek and find the will of God in the disposition of his life for the salvation of his soul." But the best lesson Xavier taught me was that all this generosity and idealism is unleashed not by abstract principles but by love, personal love — for the Lord above all, but, under him, for the human instrument who is "the father of my soul." As I lived out my life as a Jesuit and my ministry as a spiritual director, I could understand why Xavier urged Ignatius to send to the missions only those who could lead by love and not "by strictness or servile fear." I was ready to hear John of the Cross exhort the spiritual director to be firm but gentle, to encourage and support rather than to threaten. I realized that we do, indeed, catch more flies by honey than by vinegar.

But what, you might ask, does all this have to do with drinking from a dry well? Doesn't Xavier's devotion to Ignatius suggest precisely the kind of "attachment" that John and Ignatius both warn us against? It might seem that way at first glance. But Xavier, because of his love for Ignatius, was able to leave Europe and spend the last eleven years of his life as an uprooted wanderer in the Orient. That he felt it keenly is clear from the many references in his letters to the fact that he never expected to see Ignatius again in this life. He also lamented that, after four years in India, he had received only one letter from Rome (where Ignatius was) and only two from Lisbon. He felt sure that Ignatius and his brother Jesuits were writing, but travel and communication were so problematic in those days that very few of their letters ever reached him. I know how I feel today when letters from the United States take three weeks or a month (instead of the usual ten days) to reach Manila, and when, two or three times a year, a letter is lost in transit. Xavier had been exhorted by Ignatius to write often and at length about every detail of his missionary life. How painful it must have been for him to learn of Ignatius' election as the first Superior General of the Jesuits only two and a half years after the event! And to realize, as he lay dying near Hong Kong, that he would never see Ignatius or Europe again. Ignatius' letter, instructing him to come home for renewal and consultation, was still on its way to him when he died.

Xavier loved Ignatius deeply. But it was a love that led him to leave Ignatius, not to cling to him and to the joy of his presence. It has been said many times that the high point, the contemplative peak, of the Spiritual Exercises is Ignatius' fourth great thematic meditation: the three kinds of humility. He places it at the end of the second week, when the retreatants have come to a clear realization of the Lord's call to them at this moment of their lives. For Ignatius (as for Teresa and all the saints) humility is truth. The "humble" person is not one who "puts herself down," who denies the gifts and talents and loves which the Lord has given her. Rather, she is the one who recognizes all these as gifts. She knows clearly what comes from her and what from God. She lives in the truth: What do we have that we have not received? And as this realization grows in her, not only does mortal sin seem unthinkable (the first kind of humility), but even deliberate venial sin (the second kind). Realizing deeply that everything is gift, she sees *any* deliberate rejection of the Giver as gross ingratitude. That is not the end of her story though. There is another, "most perfect" kind of humility, which Ignatius proposes as the ideal culmination of gospel spirituality.

It consists in this. If we suppose the first and second kind attained, then whenever the praise and glory of the Divine Majesty would be equally served, *in order to imitate and be in reality more like Christ our Lord*, I desire and choose poverty *with Christ poor*, rather than riches; insults *with Christ loaded with them* rather than honors; I desire to be accounted as worthless and a fool *for Christ*, rather than to be esteemed as wise and prudent in this world. *For so Christ was treated before me*" (*Spiritual Exercises*, #167).

As I pointed out in *A Vacation With the Lord*, the words I underlined above are crucial to a correct understanding of Ignatius' third kind of humility. The point is not choosing poverty, insults, and contempt as values in themselves. They are not. Human nature naturally, and rightly, recoils from them.

When Francis Xavier made the Spiritual Exercises long ago in Paris, Ignatius was not exhorting him to choose exile and isolation and frustration for their own sake, out of some masochistic ideal of holiness. No; the key words are "like Christ," "for Christ," "in order to be more like Christ our Lord" who was thus "treated before me." For the person of the third kind of humility — the culminating point of Ignatius' apostolic mysticism — the supreme truth is that Jesus Christ has loved me unto death. I can only be truly humble, live in this truth, by being with him *wherever he is*. Humility is truth. And *the* truth is love: his love for me "unto the end," and the return of love that unites me totally with him. Because Xavier realized this so clearly (and that, not his journeys to the end

81

of the earth, is what made him a saint), his love for Ignatius, "the father of my soul," was not an "attachment," an obstacle to his consuming love for Christ.

Loving and Liking

In the chapters to follow, we want to explore the process by which an Ignatian apostle "grows into" the third kind of humility. Ignatius says we can "desire to attain it." We cannot choose it in the sense of making it true, of realizing it by our own efforts or desires. We can only "beg our Lord to deign to choose us for this third kind of humility" (#168). How does he deign to choose us? I think we will see that the process is closely akin to that which John of the Cross has described. But for Ignatius, the darkness is not only in prayer but also "in the marketplace" of our active lives. Since Ignatian spirituality is apostolic, it is to be expected that the action dimension of his "contemplative in action" ideal should loom large, not only in the sense that active involvement in the world is valued, but also in the deeper sense that this very involvement becomes the "sandpaper" of our sanctification.

There is one aspect of this process of apostolic purification that we should mention in this chapter, by way of conclusion and transition. Xavier loved Ignatius deeply. And, strange as it sounds, he also *liked* Ignatius. Too often we equate loving and liking — to our grief. The superiors and companions whom we can love as Xavier loved Ignatius will be few and far between in any person's life. Yet Jesus commands us to love *all* men and women, and particularly to "love one another," our brothers and sisters in the faith. What does he really mean? Is he saying that we should feel for every person the devoted love of a Xavier for an Ignatius? This might be ideal, but one does not have to live very long to realize that it is humanly impossible in this life. We are all such diverse personalities.

Temperaments clash. Even committed servants of the Lord have different perceptions of what is most important in his service. None of us can embrace the whole elephant or incarnate the whole gospel in one short life.

To resolve this dilemma we have to make a distinction, in contemporary terminology, between loving and liking. It is a distinction which I find myself explaining very often in my work of spiritual direction. To *like* other people is to feel good about them, to enjoy their company, to be "kavibes" (on the same wavelength) in Filipino idiom. In suggesting criteria for choosing a spiritual director, I have stressed that this compatibility of personality is an important criterion. Not every good director is good *for me*. I need someone with whom I am comfortable, who understands me and resonates with what I am feeling.

By contrast, the "love" of which Jesus speaks is not a question of *felt* compatibility. If it were, what would he mean by commanding us to "love your enemies"? In the Sermon on the Mount, the great compendium of Jesus' teaching on Christian discipleship, he tells us:

> "You have heard that it was said, 'You shall love your neighbor and hate your enemy.' But I say to you, Love your enemies and pray for those who persecute you, so that you may be sons [and daughters] of your Father in heaven; for he makes his sun rise on the evil and the good, and sends rain on the just and the unjust" (Mt 5:43–45).

What is he commanding us? Surely not to feel good about the fact that others persecute us. "Love" here is not a question of the feelings but of the will. That is, we should sincerely desire the good of all men and women — those who like us *and* those who dislike us, even those who hate us. Unless we

83

are masochists, we cannot *like* all people. But we can — and must — love them. We must desire their good, their salvation, their happiness here and hereafter.

Is this easy to do? After forty years in religious life and fifty-eight years on this earth, it seems clear to me that it is not easy. In fact, it seems impossible if we are left to our own resources. Jesus acknowledges that painful fact. He concludes his teaching on love of enemies with these words:

> "For if you love those who love you, what reward have you? Do not even tax collectors do the same? And if you salute only your brethren, what more are you doing than others? Do not even Gentiles do the same? You, therefore, must *be perfect* as your heavenly Father is perfect" (Mt 5:46–48).

You must be like God. And this, as we said in Part One, is impossible if we rely on our own strength to accomplish it. We must "be made perfect" (in the theologically more accurate translation of The New American Bible). The Lord has to transform us, to enable us to love all people as he loves us and them — to love even those we don't like.

So Francis Xavier was extraordinarily blessed to have known Ignatius, the father of his soul and a true friend. We all need such friends who image God's love and acceptance to us. They give us the courage to risk loving a God we cannot see, "for one who does not love his brother whom he has seen, cannot love God whom he has not seen" (1 Jn 4:20). But there will not be many such soul-friends in a person's life. All too often we will have to love those we do not find it easy to like, and sometimes those we find it extremely difficult to like, even among people with whom we share much of our lives.

This is when the third kind of humility becomes a real and awesome ideal for the true disciple of Jesus. Can I really love — sincerely desire the good of — those whom I find it hard to like and who make clear their dislike for me? Only if the process described by John of the Cross as the "dark night of the soul" has so bonded me to the Lord that my whole desire is to be "with Christ" wherever he is — even in poverty, insults, and contempt. In the end, John of the Cross and Ignatius Loyola speak the same language.

5. To Labor With Christ

Ordering Means to End

In the past ten years, I have often said that my own personal favorite among the books I have written is *Darkness in the Marketplace*. It is a difficult choice, since each of them reflects a special part of my own faith journey. But I think I favor *Darkness* because it represents and embodies my own struggle to integrate the "inner" and the "outer" aspects of my own apostolic-contemplative vocation. The apostle who seeks to grow in his or her vocation inevitably lives in dynamic tension — between personal love for God and service of his people. This is a tension that already appears in St. Paul's letters; for example, in Philippians:

> It is my eager expectation that I shall not be at all ashamed, but that with full courage now as always Christ will be honored in my body, whether by life or by death. For to me to live is Christ, and to die is

gain. If it is to be life in the flesh, that means fruitful labor for me. Yet which I shall choose I cannot tell. I am hard pressed between the two. My desire is to depart and to be with Christ, for that is far better. But to remain in the flesh is more necessary on your account (Phil 1:20–24).

In Paul's case the tension is healthy, because Jesus Christ has become the real center of his life. To be with Christ wherever he is: That is the animating principle of every decision Paul makes. But, as we have seen earlier, this kind of centering love does not come easily to us human beings. Even in the cloister, as John of the Cross makes clear, only gradually and painfully does the dark night purify us of our attachments to those other goods that compete with God for the center of our hearts. What of those of us who live our lives "in the world"? Is this centering on God alone easier or more difficult for us? My sense is that it is neither easier nor more difficult; it is *equally difficult* whatever our state of life, whether cloistered or apostolic, religious or lay, married or single.

In guiding a retreatant in choosing a state of life during the second week of the Spiritual Exercises, St. Ignatius says that we must consider "the intention of Christ our Lord, and, on the other hand, that of the enemy of our human nature" (#135). Then he adds: "Let us also see how we should prepare ourselves to arrive at perfection in whatever state or way of life God our Lord may grant us to choose." "Perfection" is the goal. Whatever state of life will best lead *me* to perfection — to the total love and service of God our Lord, as Ignatius often expresses it more concretely — is the one I should choose. No one vocation is best for every person. What is important is what is best *for me*, what is God's will for me.

Thus what matters for Ignatius is not *what* I choose but *why* I choose it. At the end of the second week (#169 ff.)

he gives guidelines for "making a choice of a way of life." And he begins by reiterating the "Principle and Foundation" (#23) with which the retreatant began the retreat. At that time it was an ideal, a guiding principle that the retreatant hoped to make his or her own as the Exercises unfolded. Now, Ignatius hopes, it should be the retreatant's felt conviction and desire. He says:

> In every good choice, as far as depends on us, our intention must be simple. I must consider only the end for which I am created, that is, for the praise of God our Lord and for the salvation of my soul. Hence, whatever I choose must help me to this end for which I am created.

Only in that spirit and with that disposition can I make a good, single-hearted, God-centered choice.

But such a disposition is not very common, whether in marriage or in the religious life. As Ignatius goes on to say, "I must not subject and fit the end to the means, but the means to the end. Many first choose marriage, which is a means, and secondarily the service of God our Lord in marriage, though the service of God is the end." They have things backwards. They choose to marry Joe for natural reasons: romantic attraction, security, escape from a difficult home situation. Then, having chosen the means (marrying Joe) already, they seek to serve God (the end) with this predetermined means. And Ignatius implies that it is not only those who marry who get things backwards. He goes on to say: "So also others first choose to have benefices (endowed ecclesiastical positions, with a stable income and status, which were common in his time), and afterwards to serve God in them." Benefices are rare in our day, but one can still choose religious or priestly life for security or prestige or to escape a challenging situation "in the world."

One can also choose a celibate life because it is nobler, more perfect, "holier." Here the deception is more subtle, since these appear to be loftier motives. But the problem remains: In doing so, I choose what *I* think God must prefer. I don't ask *him*. As Ignatius says, I still "make of the end a means, and of the means an end." I should rather choose what is right for me, not what seems better in itself; that is, "my first aim should be to serve God, which is the end, and only after that, if it is more profitable (more conducive to my end) to have a benefice or to marry, for these are means to the end."

Thus it appears that, for Ignatius, it is equally difficult to make a good initial choice of a state of life, whether we choose the lay life or the religious life. I think this is confirmed by my own experience as a teacher. In the course on discernment, when I discuss Ignatius' teaching concerning making a good, God-centered choice, my married students look quite uncomfortable. When I ask them to share their own experience, almost all say they feel they did choose the means (marriage) first. My religious and clerical students are more ambivalent: Several would say that their initial motives in choosing a celibate vocation were more in accord with Ignatius' ideal. I have come to doubt, however, that there is any real difference here. As I reflect on their sharings over the years, it seems to me that it is the *younger* religious (and my religious students do tend to be younger than those in lay life) who feel most confident about their initial motivation! Those who have lived longer with their choice (religious or lay) are much less sure of the rightness of their own initial intentions. The honeymoon idealism of their earlier years has given way to a more realistic self-knowledge and a more sober self-doubt.

This is an important insight in the context of our present discussion. We are exploring the ways one learns to live gracefully in the dry well, and the ways in which this dryness or darkness, whether in prayer or in our active lives, conforms us — gradually, as John of the Cross has made clear — to God. Ignatius was a realist. He knew that we do not complete the work of transformation even in a good thirty-day retreat. How often my seminarians, aglow with the experience of a real retreat encounter with the Lord, are brought crashing back to earth soon after. And how many others, religious and lay, come to mistrust their retreat experience because they have had real depth experiences and made good, generous resolutions, and yet later "nothing has changed."

I said that Ignatius was a realist. His apostolic ideal has been beautifully expressed in the phrase *instrumentum conjunctum cum Deo*. That is, the true apostle should be "an instrument shaped to the hand of God." I am left-handed and large handed. Some ballpens are very comfortable for me to use, and some are painfully ill-shaped to my large left hand. As a bachelor I have to do some sewing and mending for myself. The sewing kit I use contains a scissors which must have been made for midget fingers. It is painful to use and difficult to remove once it is wedged onto my fingers. Many (all?) of us are like the troublesome ballpen and scissors. God can cut and sew with us, but we are not well-shaped to his hand. We pinch and gouge and make his work more difficult. And, as both Ignatius and John of the Cross realized fully, it takes a lifetime of purifying transformation for us to be truly shaped to his hand. In fact, at this stage of my life it sometimes strikes me as a pity that, by the time we *are* conformed to the contours of his loving hand, we are too old to be of much use!

Obedience: Fixing Our Eyes on God

It would seem, then, that it takes most of a lifetime to achieve true centering on God alone. We noted in Chapter Four that for Ignatius the ideal and goal of the apostolic life is the third kind of humility: the lived desire to be with Christ *wherever* he is, even in poverty, insults, and contempt. We don't desire these hardships in themselves any more than he did. His prayer in the garden makes clear that, humanly, he recoiled from rejection and persecution: "And going a little farther he fell on his face and prayed, 'My Father, if it be possible let this cup pass from me.'" But what mattered most to him was being united to the Father, whatever the cost. And so he concludes his prayer, "nevertheless not as I will but as you will" (Mt 26:39). I noted elsewhere (in *A Vacation With the Lord*, Day 7) that it would be foolish and dangerous to seek to be holier than Jesus. We don't desire suffering any more than he did. We do desire to be *with him* in his suffering — and in his glory.

Even this desire is a sign of great and mature love. In the honeymoon fervor of youth we may think we love the Lord totally. But, as we have seen earlier, the honeymoon ends. And then we realize how much of self there is even in our most generous desires. That is where the dark night or the dry well enters in: It is the means whereby God prepares and disposes us for "divine union." In the apostolic, action-oriented mysticism of Ignatius, this dryness or darkness makes us fit instruments (*instrumenta conjuncta*), men and women of the third kind or degree of humility. To the extent that the desire to be with Christ wherever he is has come to possess our souls, we are truly united with him in his work of saving and transforming the world. Both John and Ignatius speak of "detachment," of being *free from* all our disordered attachments in order to be *free for* God and his will. John puts it poetically: The bird's tethers (be they large ropes or tiny threads) must be cut if it is to be free to soar to God. And he sees the prayer experience of the dark night as the essential means whereby the bonds are cut. Ignatius agrees. Given his apostolic charism, however, he also stresses the value of what I have called "marketplace darkness" in setting us free. And, while I have described the tension between loving and liking as one essential element of this marketplace darkness (particularly considering the priority Ignatius gives to persons rather than to projects), the central notion in Ignatius' own vision of apostolic purification is "obedience."

The importance he gives to obedience is evidenced in the *Spiritual Exercises* by Ignatius' stress on the ways we can make a good (i.e., God-centered and God-inspired) choice. Also, living in the age of the Reformation, he appends to the *Exercises* a famous set of "Rules for Thinking With the Church" (#352–370). He says: "The following rules should be observed to foster the true attitude of mind we ought to have in the Church militant." In the rules that follow he treats of religious practices which "we should praise" (#2–9) and theological questions, such as positive vs. scholastic theology, predestination vs. free will, love vs. fear of God (#11–18) with which we should not be too preoccupied in our preaching and teaching. In both cases — religious practices and theological disputes — he gives us a picture of the issues that divided the church in the sixteenth century. His point is not to suppress legitimate discussion but to avoid confusing and dividing the people whom we serve. He says, for example: "We should not make it a habit of speaking much of predestination. If somehow at times it comes to be spoken of, it must be done in such a way that the people are not led into any error. They are sometimes misled into saying: 'Whether I shall be saved or lost has already been determined, and this cannot be changed by my actions whether good or bad.' So they become indolent and neglect the works that are conducive to the salvation and spiritual progress of their souls" (#16).

Very few preachers are tempted to "speak much" of predestination today; if they did, very few of their hearers would know what to make of it. But Ignatius' guiding principle is as valid now as it ever was: Our apostolic goal should be the good of the people we serve. That is the end. The practices we promote and the topics we discuss are but means to that end, and so should be chosen insofar as they contribute to it. Moreover, *rancorous* division within the church will only lead, pastorally, to confusion. I like to see myself as reasonably progressive on many religious questions today. But I can still see the value, as Ignatius did, of St. Paul's earlier admonition to the Corinthians not to let the gifts (tongues, prophecy, etc.) become a source of division. "For God is not a God of confusion but of peace" (1 Cor 14:33).

Thus I would see three of Ignatius' rules as crucial hinges, guiding principles for a true spirit of obedience in the ministry. In #1 he says: "We must put aside all judgment of our own, and keep the mind ever ready and prompt to obey in all things the true Spouse of Christ our Lord, our holy Mother, the hierarchical Church." Is he suggesting that we become unthinking robots? Taken by itself, the above rule might give that impression. But let us place it beside #10:

> We should be more ready to approve and praise the orders, recommendations, and way of acting of our superiors than to find fault with them. Though some of the orders, etc., *may not have been praiseworthy*, yet to speak against them, *either when preaching in public or when speaking before the people*, would rather be the cause of murmuring and scandal than of profit. As a consequence, the people would become angry with

their superiors, whether secular or spiritual. But . . . it
may be profitable to discuss their bad conduct with
those who can apply a remedy.

The lines I emphasized make two points clear: first, that some
of our superiors' actions "may not have been praiseworthy,"
and that I recognize them as such. I am not gullible or robotic
in my reactions. Second, the context Ignatius has in mind is
"when preaching in public or in speaking before the people."
His concern is pastoral. I may need to speak up, to disagree,
in the right place at the right time. But I don't wish to do
more harm than good by my indiscriminate dissent.

No community can survive without a principle of unity.
For a religious community such as the church, this involves
common customs, traditions, and rites. But it also entails the
bond of legitimate authority. Abuses are always possible (always present?) in our sinful human situation. Ignatius' whole
vision, however, is grounded on the conviction that more than
sinful humanity is involved here. The church is God's work.
It is the Body of Christ. Hence he can say:

If we wish to proceed securely in all things, we must
hold fast to the following principle: What seems to me
white, I will believe black *if the hierarchical Church
so defines.* For I must be convinced that in Christ our
Lord, the bridegroom, and in His spouse, the Church,
only one Spirit holds sway, which governs and rules
for the salvation of souls.

There are relatively few points of doctrine that the hierarchical church defines. Hence it is a rare occasion when I will
have to believe black what seems to me white. But Ignatius
is really more concerned with a basic attitude: that I surrender my own will and my judgment to the Lord working in
his church, "in order that (as he tells his Jesuit sons in their

Constitutions, Part III, #18) being united among themselves by the bond of fraternal charity, they may be able better and more efficaciously to apply themselves in the service of God and the aid of their fellow men and women."

The church is a community, a family. And no family can survive if each member goes off on his or her own. Hence if we believe in the value of unity, we are prepared to sacrifice something of our own autonomy for the good of the whole, for the well-being of the community itself, and also (a crucial point in Ignatius' apostolic vision) for the sake of the *corporate* ministry to which we are called. We could also affirm the same principle of any democratic state or service organization, or even of any business enterprise. What is unique here, of course, is the faith dimension: the conviction that it is really *God* to whom we surrender our autonomy. Hence my obedience is not just a matter of practicality or efficiency. And the focus of it is not the community (the church) or its leaders (however wise or efficient they may be), but the Spirit of God who "I must be convinced. . . holds sway, Who governs and rules for the salvation of souls both in Christ our Lord, the bridegroom, and in His spouse the Church."

It is God himself to whom I surrender my will and my judgment. Once I forget that crucial fact I risk a real crisis of faith. Ignatius makes this point clearly in the Jesuit Constitutions, in a homey and down-to-earth context. He says that if one is sent to help the cook in the kitchen, he should obey wholeheartedly.

> For if he does not do this, neither, it seems, would he show obedience to any other superior, since genuine obedience considers, not the person to whom it is offered, but Him for whose sake it is offered; and if it is exercised for the sake of our Creator and Lord alone, then it is the very Lord of everything who is

obeyed. . . . For to consider the matter with sound understanding, obedience is not shown either to those persons or for their sake, but to God alone and only for the sake of God our Creator and Lord (the *General Examen*, chapter 4, #29).

Discernment in the Dry Well

My point in the preceding section is that obedience is the marketplace correlate of the dark night of prayer. In both cases we "see by faith alone," particularly as we mature and learn to live gracefully in the dry well. It is only logical to expect, then, that obedience will not be easy, any more than persevering in the dark night is easy, even if we are clear, intellectually, that it is God we obey and not human beings. I often recall a common saying from my early years as a Jesuit. Celibacy, we were told by our elders, is the most difficult vow when you are young; but, as you grow older, obedience is much more difficult. In my youth I could not imagine that this was true. That is, celibacy was clearly the most difficult then, and seemed likely to remain such as long as I lived! Whatever challenges obedience might present, I could not imagine it becoming more challenging than celibacy.

I am older and wiser now. Celibacy remains a challenge. But a certain healthy realism tempers the struggle. I have learned better how to manage my instinctual nature. And my years in the ministry have made clear to me that marriage, if lived maturely and well, is just as difficult as celibacy could ever be. Moreover, I find myself thinking as my sunset years approach: God help any woman who married me now! By contrast, obedience has become more difficult. When I was young I did not know the reasons why my superiors made the decisions they did. Why was I suddenly sent to the Philippines after years of preparing for the mission in Japan? I had no idea, and no one told me. But that was a minor problem, at worst, since I assumed that my superiors, older and wiser than I, knew much more than I did about the situation. Now I am older myself — and wiser, at least, than *I* was thirty-five years ago. My provincial superior and my rector are now about fifteen years younger than I am. And I know that they are fallible human beings, with their own personality types and their own particular blind spots. There are even situations now where I *know* that they do not know more about the matter in question than I do. It is still easy enough to obey where the decisions made don't touch my own life directly and immediately, where I do not know "all the facts." But when the matter in question touches my own areas of competence (including my own self, whom I know much better now), then obedience is clearly most difficult.

That is why I can now appreciate better Ignatius' stressing that it is the Lord we obey. I have had to undergo a real purification, akin to the dark night, of my motivation for obeying. Human nature rebels, as it does in the darkness of prayer, and I have had to learn to center more and more on the Lord's will in the decisions of ecclesiastical and religious superiors. John's "loving attentiveness" to God and his working applies equally well in this marketplace area of my life. And just as much faith is demanded. Inevitably, there have been times over the past twenty years when I could not understand what God was doing, or even see that decisions made and policies adopted were his doing. That has not always been the case, thank God. Just as John tells us there are oases of light and consolation in the dark night (cf. *Dark Night*, I, 14, #5; and II, 19, #3–4), so too there are bright spots and good times in my apostolic life. But the dark times are not only the most challenging; they are also the most productive of real purification and transformation.

There is another sense, too, in which obedience becomes more challenging and more transforming. If it is really God whom I obey, then I cannot just follow blindly what any human being thinks to be his will. That is, as I explained in *Weeds Among the Wheat*, authority can give the general guidelines for the church or the community. But, as St. Thomas pointed out long ago, it cannot dot all the "i"s or cross all the "t"s. Obedience can assign me to the Philippines as spiritual director at San Jose Diocesan Seminary, but it cannot spell out how I should deal with each seminarian whom I direct, with his own unique history and personality. That is where discernment enters in. I have to "sense" (to discern) when is the right time to confront and challenge him, when to support him gently. I have to discover his own generosity and respect his freedom.

It is striking that St. Ignatius, with his distinctive emphasis on obedience in the apostolic life, is also renowned for his teaching on discernment. The director in the Spiritual Exercises is not just, or even primarily, an authority figure. He or she, in fact,

> ought not to urge the retreatant more to poverty or any promise than to the contrary, nor to one state of life or way of living more than to another. . . . Therefore, the director of the Exercises, as a balance at equilibrium, without leaning to one side or the other, should permit the Creator to deal directly with the creature, and the creature directly with her Creator and Lord (#15).

Ignatius says that, outside of retreat, it may be legitimate to suggest or endorse a certain choice. But the retreat is a privileged time and an ideal situation for the retreatant to discern directly the Lord's will for her. The director's task is to be a co-discerner, an interpreter of the retreatant's experience of God and of his call to her.

Thus, whereas authority provides the general guidelines for following God's will in our lives, direction and discernment are more concerned with the concrete and existential dimension of personal commitment. Both are necessary: the former, because we come before God as a community, because we serve and love him as parts of the one articulated body, the church; and the latter, because each of us is personally committed to him in a unique relationship of love. Indeed, one important aspect of the marketplace darkness in our lives is the tension inevitably involved in balancing community and personal call, obedience to legitimate human authority and discernment. As always, it is easier to emphasize one to the neglect of the other. But real maturity and growth comes only from living the tension involved in keeping the two in dynamic balance in our lives. And this requires deep faith, real loving attentiveness to the Lord working *both* through authority and through personal call.

Fortunately, though, it is possible here too (as well as in prayer) to come to be at home in the dry well. Just as we can learn to be at peace in the dark night of prayer, so too we can live peacefully with the obscurity of God's call in our active lives. In chapter 9 of *Weeds Among the Wheat* I reflected on what it means to mature in discernment. Gradually discernment as formal process (the step-by-step evaluation of our consolations and desolations outlined by Ignatius) gives way to the *habit* of discerning love. It is similar to what happens to a couple who have lived long together in a good marriage. At the beginning they do not know how to read the feelings and desires of each other. There are many misunderstandings. They have to "level" with each other, each telling the other what he or she really felt or meant. But as time passes in a good marriage, they develop a "sixth sense" for what the other person is feeling. There is nothing magical about this. It simply means that they can read the signs — a small gesture, a tone of voice — that they would not have noticed earlier. Often they don't even have to look for signs, however subtle. They simply know from past experience that the spouse does not like this kind of thing or does like that. The wife who is still trying to force her husband to like parsnips or turnips after thirty years of serving them and listening to his complaints, is a pretty obtuse wife!

The habit of discernment is like that. The Lord is the spouse, and gradually we develop a sense for what pleases him and what does not. It is not easy, since God's preferences do not always correspond to ours. And, no matter how long we live, we never fully understand why God prefers what he does. For example, why do good people suffer? If the "good people" in question are not very close to us, we can give ourselves a theological explanation: God does not *desire* suffering; he only permits it. But why, if God is all-powerful and all-good, does he even permit it? Perhaps, we say (at least *I* say), because he has given us freedom, and the suffering in the world is the result of our abuse of that freedom. If God forced us to be good — if he constantly intervened to protect us and others from the consequences of our abuse of freedom — then we would no longer be free. And if we were not free to reject love, then neither would we be free to love, to do good. Love, if it is genuine, must be freely given. But that means, necessarily, that it can be freely rejected or abused.

That line of reasoning has brought me insight and peace over the years. As I said above, however, it works much better if I do not know the sufferers involved personally. It brings me more peace if the question involves the famine victims of Ethiopia and the Sudan, whom I have never met. It is less convincing if the suffering is in my own family, or my own seminary community, or among the Filipino people I love and work with. That is, my *head* is still convinced by the same argument, but my *heart* is much more likely to rebel. What really brings me a dark peace here is my own experience of the Lord. He has been faithful in the past, in *my* past. He has written straight with my crooked lines. The remembrance of the many times he has done so, more than any logical or theological argument, is the basis of my trust in the present and for the future. It is the history of his dealings with me, lovingly remembered, which convinces me that "in everything God works for good with those who love him, who are called according to his purpose" (Rom 8:28).

All Things in God

It is possible, then, to learn to live gracefully and happily in the dark night, not only in prayer, but also in our active "marketplace" lives. Both darknesses are part of the one process of purification and transformation whereby the Lord unites us to himself. As John of the Cross pointed out, however, there is both an active night and a passive night involved in the darkness of prayer. Similarly, the dark purification of our life of service will be primarily God's work (the passive night), but it does demand our cooperation (the active night). In the apostolic life, too, many enter the dark night but very few persevere until the end. The idealism of our early years is clouded by disappointment, lack of appreciation, the experience of human frailty in ourselves and in those we serve. Mid-life crises are a part of almost every marriage, and "burnout" is a common phenomenon in the apostolic ministry.

When these crises arise, our generosity is sorely tested. The temptation to lose our nerve, to decide to give up in a time of desolation, is very strong. Most committed disciples of the Lord do not give up entirely. But, like John's prayers, they settle for a level of comfortable mediocrity. They carve out for themselves a niche in which they can live and serve without being too much disturbed by others or by their own frailty. Like Ignatius' second kind of person — and we can see here why his second week meditation on the three kinds or classes of persons is so important — they bargain with the Lord: They give him *something*, but not what *he* desires. They do serve him, but within the limits their own timidity has set on his claim to their love and service. Is this bad? Not entirely. There is genuine love for the Lord here, and he will surely bless them for what they have been able to give of themselves. But it is a sad situation, considering what might have been. And, as I pointed out in chapter 5 of the *Well*, it simply postpones until purgatory the work of purifying transformation which the Lord wished to accomplish in this life.

John of the Cross said that the dark night is purgatory, understood as a time of transformation, not of punishment. If we refuse to cooperate with the Lord's purifying fire, we delay the day of full union with him. And when we die and see clearly what we have refused, we will say with St. Augustine (but with greater remorse since we have delayed longer), "Too late have I loved Thee, O Beauty ever ancient, ever new." In the life of the apostle, moreover, there is another dimension to the tragedy of our timidity. Not only do we fail to love the Lord as we are loved. We also fail to become "instrumenta conjuncta," instruments shaped to the hand of God. We work *for* him, but we cannot do *his* work, because we have set limits to what he can do in and through us.

What, though, of those who desire not to set limits, who want to cooperate fully with the Lord in the marketplace darkness whereby he makes them fit instruments of his love for others? It is for them that Ignatius composed his *Spiritual Exercises*, and John his *Ascent* and *Dark Night*. It is for them

— for you — that I write now. How do we cooperate with the Lord's purifying work in us? The general principle is the same as that given by John for pray-ers in the dark night: Center totally on God, and let go of all else when the Lord takes it away. My projects, my ideas of how best to serve, my expectations of others — all of these are but means. They are not bad. In fact, they are good and necessary, since we are called to cooperate actively in the work of redemption. But we should not clutch them, cling to them. Our grip on them should be loose and relaxed, so that the Lord can change or remove them whenever he wishes.

Ignatius realized that this kind of spiritual freedom is not fully achieved in a retreat — even a thirty-day retreat. In the next chapter we will consider some of the means he gives us for cooperating with God as he builds on the good foundation of the retreat. Here, though, we might note that Ignatius ends the *Exercises* with a "Contemplation to Attain the Love of God." It seems that he intended this exercise as a link between the retreat and the daily life to which we then return. The grace is "to ask for an intimate knowledge of the many blessings received, that filled with gratitude for all, I may in all things love and serve the Divine Majesty." During the days following the retreat, by praying over God's work as creator, dwelling in and working through all his creatures and making them sharers in his own divine goodness and being, I seek to deepen my commitment to "love and serve the divine majesty in all things." The good beginning of a generous retreat needs to be deepened and consolidated as the days and years pass. While he focuses in his Spiritual Exercises on the essential "good beginning," Ignatius was quite as convinced as John that the work of transformation in God is a lifetime process.

The story is told that, in his later years, Ignatius was asked how long it would take him to accept the suppression of his beloved Society of Jesus — not at all a remote possibility in those early days, when a non-monastic religious order was a strange and, for many, anomolous innovation in the life of the church. His answer, as recorded by his disciples, was "About fifteen minutes." Even the Society, close as it was to Ignatius' heart, was but a means to the glory of God. The very fact that it would have taken him all of fifteen minutes to come to peace about its suppression revealed how dear it was to him. I feel sure that, in the years that remained to him, he was struggling to reduce that fifteen minutes to a much shorter time. All that really mattered was "the end for which I am created, that is, for the praise of God and for the salvation of my soul" (*Spiritual Exercises*, #169).

6. The Prayer of the Apostle

John Complements Ignatius

The "Contemplation to Attain the Love of God" is intended, as we have seen, as a transition from the retreat experience of the Spiritual Exercises to our day-by-day life of service and love. As Ignatius says in the first pre-note to this contemplation, "love ought to manifest itself in deeds rather than in words." Talk is cheap, if it is not incarnated in our way of loving and acting. The second pre-note spells out the "deeds" dimension of the retreatant's commitment to the Lord (and of the Lord's commitment to the retreatant): "Love consists in a mutual sharing of goods; for example, the lover gives and shares with the beloved what he possesses . . . and vice-versa, the beloved shares with the lover."

In the preceding chapter we have considered the most important aspects of this mutual sharing of gifts. The Lord gives us himself in love; we in turn give him ourselves in love, not only for him but for all those he has commanded us to love as he loves them — and because he loves them. In Chapter Four, we saw both the beauty and the cost of our gift (when our loves and our "likes" do not coincide). Similarly, we indicated in Chapter Five that obedience, as love incarnated in action, is the solid core of our apostolic love for the Lord. It takes great faith here to keep our vision clear; namely, that ultimately it is the Lord we obey; and that when we do obey human beings, "genuine obedience considers, not the person to whom it is offered, but him for whose sake it is offered" (Ignatius, the *General Examen*, #29). We also stressed that the very heart of obedience thus understood is discernment — or, as Ignatius calls it, "discerning love." Discernment is where prayer and action meet. It is the art of discovering in prayer how the Lord wishes us to act. Discerning love is that habitual sensitivity to the Lord's voice and desires that comes from long years of living with him in love.

In all of these areas — learning to love as we are loved, obeying "God alone and only for the sake of God," and developing the sensitivity of heart that Ignatius calls discerning love — growth is a gradual, lifelong process. And this growth inevitably involves a dry well experience closely analogous to John of the Cross' dark night of prayer. As the thematic meditations of his second week make clear, Ignatius saw the process of formation of true disciples as one of real and rigorous purification. To choose the banner of Christ ("poverty, humiliations, humility") goes against our natural desire for "riches, honors, pride." To be the third kind of person, to "make efforts neither to want that (i.e., the ten thousand 'ducats' of Ignatius' parable), nor anything else, unless the service of God alone move them to do so" — this too is alien to our natural human inclinations. It will take most of us a lifetime of purification to come to that level of loving.

I said above that the dry-well experience of apostolic purification is closely analogous to John of the Cross' dark night of prayer. It would be more accurate to say that they are essentially identical. While their perspectives differ (divine union in prayer and union of wills in service), the same total centering on God and his will is at the heart of both John's and Ignatius' teaching. In both of their spiritualities, we could say that for the true disciple and lover, whether one is a cloistered contemplative or an active apostle is really secondary. What matters is not *which* I am, but *why* I am what I am. All else is "means."

There is, moreover, a still greater similarity, or identity, between John's vision and that of Ignatius. The latter was convinced that it is precisely the apostle's life of prayer which is the crucial means to his or her apostolic transformation. This may be somewhat obscured by the fact that the Spiritual Exercises are primarily concerned with laying a good initial foundation for a life of loving service. For this reason, I have long been convinced that Ignatius' teaching and guidance needs to be complemented by that of John of the Cross. John presupposes the good beginnings of which Ignatius speaks, and then goes on to tell us how to build (or better, how the Lord builds) on this solid foundation. Thus we may find John a helpful guide in elaborating an authentically Ignatian vision of *mature* apostolic prayer. There are three key elements in this Ignatian apostolic prayer: formal mental prayer, the examination of conscience, and the retreat. Let us consider, in each of these areas, what it means to come to maturity by building on the solid initial foundation of the experience of the Spiritual Exercises.

Prayer: Waiting on a Quiet God

In directing experienced pray-ers, I find they have one recurring complaint about their prayer. It is, they tell me, filled with distractions. As we saw in Chapter Two, these distractions can be a sign of the beginner's lack of depth and experience, or of some negligence in the life of a more mature pray-er. But assuming that the person is both well-grounded and generous, then we have to conclude that the distractions are a normal, though frustrating, sign of the dry well or dark night. In that case, Teresa of Avila tells us, we should simply learn to ignore them, to realize that they are on the surface of our consciousness, whereas the Lord is working, encountering us at a deeper level "in the soul." In *When the Well Runs Dry*, I suggested that the imagination and understanding are now like the children at an adult party. They don't grasp what is going on between the adults (the soul and the Lord) and so they clamor for attention. And the more we attend to them, the more demanding they become. Like spoiled children they know they can get our attention by making trouble. On the other hand, as Teresa realized, if we ignore them they will eventually quiet down, since they learn that they don't gain anything by their antics.

In giving directees this advice, I am always reminded of my own boyhood. My mother was quite a strict disciplinarian. We had a happy life at home, and the family was really the center of our lives. But she had two boys to raise, and the two of us, as is normal, battled our way through our early years. When things got out of control, punishment was swift and firm. To my regret then, I never heard her say, "Wait till your Father gets home!" Yet, several times friends or relatives said to me, "Your mother is the most serene, ladylike person we know. She never gets angry." I used to wonder if they were talking about the same woman I knew. As I grew older, though, I realized that they were. When we were out in public, she kept her composure (as far as humanly possible) and ignored our misbehavior. But she had a mind like a computer. Everything was filed away, and the time of reckoning came as soon as we arrived home, by which time my brother and I had forgotten the misdemeanors!

This seems to me a perfect parable for the way we should handle a distracted imagination or understanding in prayer. While praying it is best to ignore them. Otherwise we will simply ruin the prayer (the communication between the adults) and spoil the children by attending too much to them. But if they are particularly demanding or obnoxious, discipline them *outside of prayer.* By means of some appropriate penance or mortification — for example, by depriving the imagination of some legitimate entertainment or recreation — make them pay the price for disrupting the prayer time. Gradually they will learn to behave better. There will always be distractions floating in and out (since our imagination is always active, even when we are asleep), but they will not be so persistent or insistent. They will become easier to ignore when we come before the Lord.

There is still the problem of those ever-present, floating distractions that come and go, one following the other without any coherence or logical sequence. As I say, they cannot be eliminated as long as the imagination is alive and active. And we don't wish to kill the imagination, only to tame it. Teresa does speak (in the Fourth Mansion of the *Interior Castle*) of a "prayer of recollection," wherein the Lord brings all the faculties to quiet and enables the pray-er to be totally centered on him. But this is a supernatural gift. And even when the Lord gives it, he does so only for a time and occasionally. Usually the distractions persist as "background noise," the reason being that we need to cooperate with the Lord by disciplining ourselves to ignore them. This is really John of the Cross' active night of sense and spirit: our cooperation with the passive night whereby the Lord tames and purifies our faculties.

What most alarms sincere pray-ers, as it did me, is that this distractedness also occurs during the celebration of the Eucharist, even at the time of the consecration and of communion. It seems to us that we should be totally recollected, at least at this peak moment of our life with the Lord. Previously we were filled with devotion during the eucharistic celebration. Now, however, these times are no less distracted than our ordinary prayer periods. Even in the Eucharist, it seems, we are asked to drink from a dry well. It is a frustrating experience. The cold comfort I can offer — cold but reassuring, if we take it to heart — is that this seems to be the normal experience of pray-ers in the dry well. Even at the Eucharist, it appears, we must learn to "let go and let God." Even here we must set aside our own expectations concerning what should be happening, what we should be feeling.

A favorite story of mine can serve as a metaphor for the Lord's apparent silence. A young couple had just one son, about six years old. He was healthy, lively, good-natured. But he had never talked. The parents took him to every kind of specialist: a doctor, a speech therapist, a psychologist. Nothing seemed to be wrong either organically or psychologically. But he never spoke. One day the family was at dinner when suddenly the little boy said, "The potatoes are cold." The parents were stunned, then ecstatic. The mother threw her arms around the youngster and exclaimed: "My son! You talked! You talked!" Then, when things quieted down, the father asked the little boy: "But why only now? If you were able to speak, why didn't you say anything before this?" And his son said, "Up till now everything was fine."

God is like that little boy. We have to learn to live with God's silence, confident that he will speak when he has anything to say. From a deeper perspective we can say with St. Teresa that God is not really silent, but we are deaf. He speaks in the "still small voice" of the Elijah story (1 Kgs 19:12), which our ears are not sensitive enough to hear. The Lord is speaking in the Eucharist, for example, but now in a deep and quiet way that, for us, is drowned out by the surface noises of our own thoughts and imaginings. The fact remains, though, that as far as we can tell the Lord is silent. We cannot hear him. He will speak audibly when we are ready. But in the meantime we have to trust that this frustrating dryness is really a sign of growth: a sign that he is taking us deeper, that the surface consolations which delighted us before can no longer satisfy us. In this sense, at least, "everything is fine."

One more observation is in order, concerning the apostolic meaning of our distractions in prayer. Sometimes they are not really distractions. That is, they may not seem to us to be part of our dialogue with the Lord, and yet they may reveal what he wants to talk to us about or make known to us. Even beginners have to learn that the Lord is not bound to *their* theme or topic. They may plan to meditate on the gospel of the day; but prayer is a dialogue, not a monologue. When I was a Jesuit novice, we were assigned to recreate in "bands" of three, and each of us was advised to prepare his topic of conversation in advance. The result was some very odd exchanges. Each novice had his own planned topic. And, often enough, we had three people talking and nobody listening! We do not want to do the same thing with the Lord. We don't want to be so fixated on *our* expectation of what should transpire in our prayer that we are not open to be surprised by him.

This is especially true in apostolic prayer. Our "distractions" will often relate to the demands of our active life. And

113

they may well not be distractions, but inspirations from him concerning our choosing and acting. What we do need to learn is how to distinguish between talking (and listening) to the Lord and talking to ourselves. If I become all wrapped in a discussion *with myself* about my problems and concerns — if the Lord is forgotten — then these concerns are real distractions. But if I bring them to him and talk to him about them — and learn to give him equal time to respond if he wishes — then they are not really side trips but the very substance of our encounter with him. This is why I, personally, have not found it helpful to try to "block out" all distractions in my prayer. Rather, as I have learned over the years, it is better to begin the prayer by surfacing all my concerns, bringing them into the prayer and then handing them over to the Lord. "Lord, these are my concerns as I come before you today. If you wish to speak to me about them, fine. But if not, let them pass away." For me at least, this is much more effective than struggling to set them aside. Usually they do fade out of consciousness. And if they don't, that presumably is the Lord's will.

What we do need, then, as good apostles is a half hour each day of real "listening" prayer. That is, a half hour given to him to do with it whatever he wishes. Ignatius does not believe a longer time is required in the apostolic life, since (in the proper sense of a much-abused expression) my work should be my prayer. Cloistered contemplatives, by the very nature of their vocation, should usually give a longer time to formal prayer. And Ignatius prescribed more for his young Jesuits in formation, since they (like a young couple courting) are still laying a solid foundation for a lifetime of loving. But for mature apostles, a half hour daily should suffice; it is necessary if we are not to get lost on the surface of our lives. What matters is the *quality* of the time we give the Lord: It should be real *listening* prayer, a time to come back to our center and to let the whole of our life and ministry come into proper focus. Our daily fidelity symbolizes and realizes (makes real) our conviction that our only end is the glory of God and the salvation of our souls, and that all else is means.

The Examen: Two Sides of the Same Hand

One of the most characteristically Ignatian practices is the examination of conscience. It was not original with Ignatius, of course, since it has solid roots in desert and monastic spirituality. But Ignatius, in the early part of the *Spiritual Exercises* (#24–44), gives a detailed plan for both a "particular" (on some specific point which we are trying to improve or correct) and a "general" examination of conscience. While it is clear (cf. #18 & 19) that he proposed this plan especially for beginners in the spiritual life, we also know that he considered it of permanent value. He himself practiced it throughout his life, and he recommended it to all his Jesuit sons.

In chapter 5 of *Opening to God* I discussed the value of the examen as a means of purification for beginners even today. I also recommended the contemporary adaptation, proposed by George Aschenbrenner, S.J., and others, known as the "consciousness examen." What, though, of Ignatius' insistence that it remain part of any mature apostolic spirituality? Specifically, what is the role of the examen once we are drinking from a dry well in our prayer? Can we still use the detailed scheme which Ignatius proposes in the Exercises, or must it be adapted to the dry well or dark night? Based on my own experience, I believe some adaptation is essential. But to understand why and how we should adapt this characteristically Ignatian practice, we should first recall its real purpose for Ignatius.

A fundamental insight of the Spiritual Exercises, as of St. John of the Cross' teaching, is that knowledge of God and knowledge of self go hand in hand. In the first week of the

Exercises we seek the grace of self-knowledge: to know and experience myself as God sees me. This is the first part of the truth that sets us free. And the examen is, for Ignatius, an essential tool precisely in the process by which I seek this painful but liberating self-knowledge. We saw in *A Vacation With the Lord* that the second week, in which we seek to know, love, and follow God in Christ Jesus, is the heart of the Spiritual Exercises. "Putting on the Lord Jesus" is the real goal of the retreat. But we can be filled with Christ only to the extent that we are emptied of ourselves and of our illusions. Hence, while the second week is the most important, the heart of the matter, we can say that the first week is the most crucial: If this first week is made well and fruitfully, the rest of the retreat will flow smoothly and almost automatically. The first week is also generally the most difficult. Honest self-confrontation is much more unpleasant and taxing than is contemplating Jesus in the gospels.

It is also true that we never know ourselves fully in this life. As I grow older, I have much more self-knowledge than I had in my youth. But the more I know, the more mysterious I am to myself. This was St. Paul's lament in Romans 7:15: "I do not understand my own actions. For I do not do what I want, but I do the very thing I hate." Thus the goal of honest self-knowledge is clearly not realized in one good retreat. If retreatants are generous and open, they will see themselves honestly to the extent, and in the way, that the Lord desires for them *at this moment* in their lives. They will acquire the self-knowledge that is necessary now, as the foundation of God's word to them in the second week. But this is just the tip of the iceberg. As he continues to reveal himself to them throughout their lives, his light will also illuminate deeper and darker recesses of their own selves. It is because Ignatius saw this process as ongoing and lifelong that he considered the examen to be an essential feature of our spirituality as long as we live. To practice the examination of conscience day by day is not a repetitive, routine activity. The point is not simply to measure myself every day against some invariable checklist of obligations and sins. Rather, each day's examen is part of an ongoing process of growth in self-knowledge and in sensitivity to the way the Lord is working in my life. It is, in essence, an exercise in discernment whose goal is an ever-greater discerning love.

Given this understanding of the Ignatian examen, perhaps it is clear that the way we practice it will necessarily evolve as we mature in prayer. Just as the detailed steps and practices of meditation and Ignatian contemplation give way to a greater receptivity or passivity in our prayer, so too the examen will become simpler, less detailed, more an exercise in listening to the Lord as *he* reveals to us who we really are. The examen, too, will become more "contemplative" in the Carmelite sense. After some years we know ourselves better. We know the areas where we are likely to fail. And we know much more "instinctively" what in us pleases or displeases the Lord. We don't need a detailed analysis of our day, or of the commandments, to spot our failings or to see where the Lord has been calling us to greater generosity.

It seems that Ignatius himself practiced the examen in some detail all of his life. In part, this may be a question of personality; he was a very methodical man. But I feel sure that the simplification I described in the preceding paragraph is also revealed in his journal. Whatever procedure he followed, the examen became simpler, more intuitive, more contemplative. And I have discovered, even though I too am a methodical person, that the examen and my formal prayer tend to fuse into a single experience. That is, more and more knowledge of God and knowledge of myself are seen as simply two sides of the same hand. In coming to know God, I inevitably come to know myself better. The more I confront his light, the clearer the contrast with my own darkness is.

This seems to be related to what I have called "writing the fifth gospel." In our early years we go to the four gospels — to Matthew, Mark, Luke, and John — to discover in meditative prayer who Jesus Christ was for the first generation of disciples. We see him, come to know and love him, through their eyes. At this time the examen, as a separate exercise, focuses our gaze on ourselves and on Jesus working in our own lives. It relates our gospel meditation to our own concrete experience of God's call to us. In this way knowledge of God in Christ Jesus is complemented (as it must be, if it is to be real and fruitful in good works) by honest self-knowledge. Gradually, however, our prayer becomes less a reflection on the gospel of Mark or Luke, and more an encounter with the Lord here and now. He seems to be asking us: "But who do *you* say that I am?" (Mt 16:15). We can no longer simply repeat the answer of Mark. His experience of Jesus, while it was the same Jesus whom John encountered, is unique and personal. Mine must be unique too. At this point the four canonical gospels become less a source of information about the historical Jesus, and more a priming of the pump of my own love for him. It is a joy to hear those who loved him speak of him because it stirs my own memories and moves my own heart. I must now "write the fifth gospel" in my own prayer and life. I must give my own answer to the question: "Who do *you* say that I am?"

Thus it is, I believe, that formal prayer and the examen tend to fuse into a single activity in the life of a mature prayer. The fifth gospel which we are writing is our answer to the question who the Lord is for us — and who we are for him. He loves us personally, in our own concrete uniqueness. The paschal mystery is not just historical fact. It is *our* story: the story of the Lord's love for us unto death, and of his conquest of death in our life. At the same time, the examen becomes a more contemplative act. That is, the focus is on the Lord's revelation to pray-ers of who we really are — of our "sinfulness" as he sees it — and on his work of transformation. We must cooperate, of course. The active night must complement the passive night. But our cooperation is a work of discerning love. We are the partners; he is the Lord of the dance. Even our growth in self-knowledge is gift, is revelation. It is the Lord who shapes us thus into his "instrumentum conjunctum," an instrument well-shaped to the work he desires to accomplish through us. Examen and prayer are two sides of the same hand.

Retreat: Seeing the Dark

In the traditional process of spiritual formation, there are three practices which I see as closely related: the examen, the monthly recollection, and the annual retreat. Properly understood, they form a series of concentric circles in the life of the beginner in prayer. Concentric, because they all have the same focal point: growth in sensitivity to the Lord at work in my life, revealing myself (and himself) to me and shaping me to his hand. In the examen I contemplate how he has been revealing himself to me in the day just past. But for the Lord my whole life is a unity, a single story of formation and transformation. From his perspective each day is not an isolated event but part of a much wider picture. We tend to be myopic, nearsighted. As has often been said, we tend to see the individual threads of the tapestry and to miss the whole picture. We view the tapestry from the back, where it is a jumble of threads and colors. Only the Lord can lead us round to see it from the front, where the light and dark threads fall into place and tell a single story.

The monthly recollection and the annual retreat help to cure our myopia. In the recollection we seek to see the month as a whole, to discover the unity of the Lord's work in us during the past thirty days. There have been good days and bad days, bright threads and dark threads. But how do they fall into place as strands of the single tapestry the Lord is weaving? In the recollection we ask the grace to see more clearly the "beautiful thing" the Lord is fashioning. "What I am doing you do not know now, but afterward you will understand" (Jn 13:7). In planning the seminary recollections at San Jose, we invite different speakers and ask them to discuss specific themes relevant to the priestly formation of the seminarians. This is helpful since it focusses their reflection on various important aspects of their lives as priests to be (for example, celibacy, social concern, solid theological knowledge, priestly brotherhood). But I always tell them that, whoever the speaker and whatever the theme, the real purpose of the recollection is the same: to discern how the Lord has been working in their lives in the past month, and how sensitively they have responded to his loving call.

Similarly, the annual retreat, the widest of the three concentric circles, has as its purpose seeing the whole year through the Lord's eyes. No two retreats are the same, since we are never precisely the same person we were a year ago. A new chapter in our fifth gospel has to be written. If we are spiritually alive and well, our answer to his question "Who do you say that I am?" will never be entirely the same as it was last year. And from his divine perspective, all these years are but chapters in a single story, the story of his lifetime love and call to us. And (at least in my experience) it is only when

I get some distance from the events in my life that I can see the divine meaning in them. I have to be patient, trusting, listening — in short, I have to be a good "contemplative" — in order to come, gradually, to see my life as the Lord sees it. This above all is grace, is revelation.

As the foregoing remarks clearly suggest, the maturing pray-er in the dry well will experience the retreat differently from the beginner. Like the examen and the recollection, it will become a more "passive," more contemplative experience as time passes. The story is told that St. Ignatius, when he was informed that some Jesuits (and others) were repeating the Spiritual Exercises — the beginning of our custom of an annual retreat —he was quite happy with this development. But he insisted that, in this case, the Exercises would have to be adapted to their present needs. They would need to select certain themes, or focus on certain graces that were relevant to their current stage of the spiritual journey. Ignatius would not have had much sympathy for the director who insists that, whatever the retreatant's habitual pattern of prayer, during the retreat he or she should "follow the text of the Spiritual Exercises." As he said at the very beginning of his *Exercises*, "We call Spiritual Exercises *every* way of preparing the soul to rid itself of all inordinate attachments and . . . of seeking and finding the will of God" (#1). What "way" is suitable once our prayer has moved into the dark night or dry well? In the first place, as I always tell my retreatants (and have to remind myself), we should expect our retreat prayer to follow essentially the same pattern as our daily prayer. If the latter is dry and dark, then most likely the retreat will be too. The Lord can surprise us. But unless and until he does, we should anticipate continuity with our habitual experience of prayer. I find the retreat a privileged time — really the best time of the year — not because anything unusual or ecstatic happens, but precisely because I am totally free to "lovingly attend" to the Lord and his work in me. This means distractions, and sometimes restlessness and misery. But it brings me to the very center of myself, my very reason for being and laboring. The anxieties and frustrations of daily life fall into place, as do the joys and successes. Nothing really matters except God and his will. Even my own sinfulness (which, John of the Cross says somewhere, is the last thing devout souls surrender to the Lord) is swallowed up in the black hole of his embrace. It should bother me precisely insofar as it bothers him — no more and no less.

I used to think of dry-well prayer as "seeing in the dark." I suppose what that really meant to me was "seeing *God* in the dark," which causes eye strain and headaches. Recently, however, it seems to me the more apt metaphor is "seeing the dark" — not straining to see *what* (or *who*) is there, but simply gazing steadily and unflinchingly into the dark itself. Since my faith-conviction is that, as John of the Cross says, the dark night is contemplation, and absence is really excessive presence, my firm hope is that one day the darkness will reveal itself as Light, when my eyes have become adjusted to it. But I expect to be dead by then! I don't have to strain for it now. I can be at peace, simply "seeing" the dark as it is at present, convinced that the more I do so, the freer he is to shape me to his love and for his glory. As the fourth-century deacon St. Ephrem, a poet, mystic, and apostle of the Syrian church, said in his *Commentary on the Diatesseron* (quoted in the *Prayer of Christians* on the sixth Sunday of ordinary time): "So let this spring (the word of God) quench your thirst, and not your thirst the spring." The spring is infinite and it will take us an eternity to drink it dry. Once we realize this, we can be at home in the dry well, confident that these years of dryness are but a brief moment in the span of eternity.

Epilogue: Take and Receive

The prayer of the apostle in the dry well, then, is essentially a "letting go and letting God." More and more God takes over the work of our transformation. Initially this is alarming for most of us, since we are accustomed to be in control of our lives. And since most apostles, whether celibate or married, are temperamentally much more Marthas than Marys, it is especially difficult for them to be good floaters in the sea of the Lord. We described this difficulty, and tried to explain the reasons for it and how to cope with it, in part II of *When the Well Runs Dry*. In the present book, intended as a sequel to the *Well*, I have suggested that we can move beyond this initial anxiety and struggle. We can become at home in the darkness and the dryness. We can, that is, learn to float, perhaps not perfectly in this life, but to a degree that brings us peace living in, and drinking from, the dry well.

In the final chapter we explored the implications of this letting go and floating for the classic Ignatian practices of an apostolic interior life: "mental" prayer, the examen, and the annual retreat. What, then, would Ignatius see as the ideal attitude or disposition of the mature contemplative in action? I think he has expressed it beautifully for us in the prayer with which he concludes the *Spiritual Exercises*. We noted earlier that the final exercise, forming a transition from the retreat itself to daily life thereafter, is his "Contemplation to Attain the Love of God." There are, he tells us, four points to be considered: first, "the blessings of creation and redemption, and the special favors I have received"; second, "how God dwells in creatures" and in me "and makes a temple of me"; third, "how God works and labors for me in all creatures"; and, finally, "to consider all blessings and gifts as descending from above... as the rays of light descend from the sun, and as the waters flow from their fountains."

In each of the four points, after considering the gracious generosity of God, Ignatius asks that I "reflect upon myself, and consider, according to all reason and justice, what I ought to offer the Divine Majesty, that is, all I possess and myself with it" (#234). Love consists in a mutual exchange of gifts. Since the Lord has given me everything, including his own life and divine nature, the only adequate response is the gift of my whole self. For one who has truly and fully experienced the grace of the Exercises, nothing less will suffice. So Ignatius concludes each of the four points with his famous prayer:

Thus, as one would do who is moved by great feeling,
I will make this offering of myself:

Take, Lord, and receive all my liberty, my memory, my understanding, and my entire will, all that I have and possess. You have given all to me. To you, O

Lord, I return it. All is yours; dispose of it wholly according to your will. Give me only your love and your grace, for this is sufficient for me.

The beauty of the prayer is evident. Yet it can be quite intimidating, especially for young retreatants. What if the Lord takes me at my word, and I lose my mind?! That is a normal reaction, as long as we don't yet really know this God of ours very well. If we are not sure what he might do, it is a great risk to entrust everything to him. But as I come to know him better, I realize that he loves me more than I love myself, and that my life (my memory, my understanding, my will) is far safer in his hands than in my own. Knowing this, I realize that the real danger is in trying to keep the control of my own life and destiny to myself.

This realization is, I believe, the surest sign of the prayer's, and the contemplative in action's, maturity. Some involuntary disordered attachments will probably remain in us as long as we live. But we know, as Dante proclaimed, that in his will is our peace. To surrender all to the Lord, to allow him to shape us into good instruments fitted perfectly to the contours of his hand, is the only choice that makes sense, for John of the Cross as well as for Ignatius Loyola. Once we realize this, the pray-er can live peacefully in the dark night, and drink gratefully from the dry well. Darkness is excessive light. Dryness is superabundant water. Death is blessed release: "to be dissolved and be with Christ." Surrender to the Truth here and now (whether my vocation be to the cloister or to service in the world) is the only way to authentic freedom.